a

reason to

love me

Daniela Svampa Cowie

ISBN 978-1-913425-35-7
Published by YouCaxton Publications 2020
YCBN: 01

First published by New Generation Publishing in 2017

YouCaxton Publications
enquiries@youcaxton. co. uk

Disclaimer
I have conveyed the events used as examples in this book from my memories and perception of them. In order to maintain their anonymity, in some instances, for both legal and safety purposes, I have changed the names of certain individuals.

Contents

Looking at her, the woman in the mirror, her reflection is staring right back at me.

'Hey you... how did we get here?' I ask; as love, melancholy, sadness, fear and pride rush through me all at once. Still staring back, a woman looking younger than her actual age, yet carrying in her an old soul, and a life of a thousand journeys...

She smiles.

Although there have been times when I'd never thought I'd say it, I am so proud of whom you have become. Woman... I love you very much.

Foreword

If I ask you to think about everyone you have ever loved, you, like most people, would not think of yourself. If you did, your own self would probably not be the first person to come to mind. Why?

For many of us, love is usually projected outwards towards others. We are taught to be kind and loving to others but rarely taught what it means to love ourselves, to treat ourselves kindly or even to put ourselves first sometimes. Our culture subconsciously reinforces self-love as borderline narcissism.

The ancient Greeks recognised the complexity of the emotion we call 'love' and did not confine it to one word. They identified seven distinct types of love, namely:

Eros: Love of the body.

Philia: Affectionate love.

Storge: Love of the Child.

Agape: Selfless Love.

Ludus: Playful Love.

Pragma: Long-lasting Love.

Philautia: Love of the Self.

I deliberately wrote philautia last because that is its usual position in terms of importance. We often forget to love ourselves.

Daniela's journey to self-love did not happen suddenly in a moment of epiphany or self-discovery; it took a life-changing experience and a healing process to finally love herself unconditionally. She is one of the lucky ones because many people never find philauntia their entire life.

I hope everyone reading this book may finally find a reason or many reasons to love themselves.

Vinette Hoffman-Jackson DTM

Radio presenter, Communications Coach and Self-Discovery coach.

Author of Did the Right Sperm Win, Books 1&2, Behind my Smile and Vinette's Vignettes.

www.321speak.co.uk

Preface

Very few people get close to know, never mind understand what really goes on with me...in me. I am not even sure *I* really know; as I question myself all of the time.

On the outside people see me as lucky, they tell me "You are so lucky! You have a lovely family, a loving husband, two successful children and a lovely home, you are beautiful, you are thin, you are such a nice person, you have it good.". They are absolutely right, I do, but it is not luck. They say it as if I have inherited this great life, not a thought or acceptance seems to run within their minds of the twisted and arduous path I have walked and lessons I have learned to make it manifest. Not a single thought, of the work, the maintenance, the questioning and re-questioning, the practicing of gratefulness and positive manifestation techniques I have done, and still do, every day to live the life I live and be this person I love.

Chapter One – An Italian Beginning

Born in a small town, on the east coast near the centre of Italy and raised on a farm in the middle of what felt like nowhere, I don't recall very much of my life before the age of five, except for a couple of major events and just a few flashes of images preceding that age. Pictures of me in places that might let me know of where I have been and people I have visited; for example, a picture of little me, a chubby curly head, bendy legged 2-year-old, standing on a beach, shoulders facing the sea, looking very cross, scared and upset. Still, there are so many, stories, incidents (funny and not so funny ones), events and situations that followed since then that maybe it's just as well that my memory is failing me or this could turn into an epic.

A little fat faced, attentive, wide-eyed baby sitting on a photographer's chair posing for a picture, I can see now just from looking at me then how I have travelled the road that I have; with curiosity, suspicion and a fierce strength and determination. All written on my face, then, in that picture.

I started my life, quite isolated from the rest of the world, in a big brick style house which I shared with my parents, my sister, my paternal grand-parents, a paternal uncle and quite a few cows (yes, not kidding, cows!). Ok not all sharing the same part of the house, the cows did live in the stable on the ground floor of the house, however, still sharing the same building.

My parents, strict from the day I was born (or so it seemed), worked very hard. Daily, they were out on our farm fields and on those of other neighbours for extra income thus I didn't see them very much through the day, mainly at meal times, when the stereo typical Italian meal setting took place. Because of this, during my younger years I was raised by my grand-parents who taught me to cook (you may think a small child age 4/5 can't reach the big pot on the cooker... it is amazing what a difference a chair or a stool can make), clean and look after our farm animals. Although not by any means rich, I had, I believe, all I needed: - fairly good health, fresh air, fresh food from the farm, a tricycle, (which I would happily ride around the house singing at the top of my voice, Italian pop songs) lots of animals to interact with and a best friend who would come to see me and play with me pretty much every day, when I'd completed all my chores.

At this young age I was very close to each member of the household, my family meant everything to me. Strict, absent, stingy with emotions my parents might have been; but my family were my world, my security the solid unit never to be undone.

Life was simple then and, reasonably safe, with the exception of falling down a well while getting the water out to make the pigs their daily food mixture or being bitten by a viper, we were so isolated that the risks we face as families today were unlikely to ever present themselves. My best friend, Romina and I would play together every day, even though she had far more toys than I had, we simply played with what our surroundings offered: - a spring metal bed base was used as a trampoline a conker tree was used for our military games, a rope over a tree branch for a swing and plenty of water and earth to create enough mush for our imaginary lunches. When my sister was in a fairly generous mood (and by that I mean, she would take time out from busying herself emotionally blackmailing me, and would now bully both, my friend and I, in a much less direct manner), she would join in the games armed with Romina's little brother, Simone, who (to Romina's horror), often was allowed to come to our house to play with us too. Then the play would grow to a much larger scale. The pigs would get shut into their individual night rooms (And I had to share a room with my parents!) and we would use the divider of the sties (the pigs' day rooms) as horses quickly to be dismounted to give way to vicious battles of words, finger shootings, medic calling and... arguments (which obviously, unless we fancied a slap, my sister would win).

From this very young age, and for a few more years to come, my summers were spent outside in the fresh air, roaming the countryside; I would explore and draw on all it had to offer. My winters would be spent for some part in bed with tonsillitis, which I would get religiously every year and the rest would be divided: - partly outside, on those cold, heavy, snowy days, when us kids would get together, get some plastic sacks fill them with hay, tie them with rope and 'ski' down the highest field on the side of the house. Most of the time the hay sack would reach the bottom before our bums would, but it was good exercise to run after it, pick it up and walk all the way back up the hill with our little legs having to get through seventy – eighty centimetres of snow. Mainly though, as the winters were so intense, I would be spending them indoors. I would be helping out in the house, cooking on the open fire, sitting at the table with my dad and my uncle making cartridges for their shotguns ready for their hunting (measuring the weight of the pellets, the gun powder and filling the cartridges) and one week in the January and February months, I would be helping out with what in Italian we call 'fare la pista'; this includes making fresh salami, sausages, and our equivalent of Parma ham after the pig has been killed. I dreaded that week of the year, it was a very traumatic time for me as hearing the squealing of the animals that were to be slaughtered was horrendous. As I recall it now, shivers run through me, I can still hear their cry clear in my mind. These are the same pigs we would get 'to know' over the year when playing in the sties and become affectionate towards. I remember on many occasions closing the door of the house sitting on the stairs, covering my ears with my hands to dampen the sounds of the screaming pigs and crying; but I knew that was part of our lives, a harsh but accepted process of events where you raised animals for food. The hunting wasn't considered sport; whatever was brought back was to be eaten or preserved.

All in all though, I then believed that my childhood days were, fairly ordinary. Even though I was made aware by other neighbours that our households way of doing things was very strict, border line child slavery. I was still quite happy though as I felt I would appreciate even more the praise that, sometimes, would come my way for jobs well done, as well as the play time opportunities.

Then the first blow, the first event (or at least the first I can remember), that set off the wheel of changes that were to come, took place.

My grand-mother passed away.

I do not remember much of how it happened or what caused her to die; all I can remember is my grand-dad sitting by the fire place, tearful, sad, shaking his head.

He just kept repeating to himself that he had lost another one (I later found out that my grandma was his second wife and that my dad's real mum had died at a much younger age). He kept asking himself out loud why he, was still alive and how would he now, get on without her. I hardly remember the funeral, I was crying and screaming so much for her loss that I wasn't allowed inside the morgue, and a packet of Oreo-like biscuits was given to me, in the car on the way home, to shut me up.

Not sure what provoked what is the next memorable experience in my life, but even though dangerous and some may scream "Social Services!" I hold it as a fond and funny memory, hence why I am sharing it with you.

I was about 5 years old, and in Italy a year away from going to school. Romina had come up to see me and as I was busy helping my grand-dad gathering wood for the winter, she joined in with the task. After a little while of being on the 'job' my friend and I decided that it was time for some refreshments and made our way back to the house to get some water. As we marched up the stairs that lead to the living/dining room, we heard my mum shout at us to get out; we were leaving dirty footprints on the floor she was just in the middle of washing. Not in any way fathomed or perturbed by this and giggling our way back down, we decided to make a detour and landed ourselves in the wine cellar. The wine cellar was on the ground floor, almost opposite the front door to the house, past the landing and the stairs; just off a tiny corridor which linked the stables and my uncle's mechanic workshop. We had to be very quiet, as my uncle was there working away and although unspoken, we both knew our intentions weren't the purest. The cellar consisted of some enormous wine barrels, the majority filled with white wine but a couple with red; if that was not enough there were also a few bell jars stacked away and in the far corner, near the cellars outside door, an old fashion wine press machine that we used every September when we harvested the grapes. The barrels had a key tap pouring mechanism for wine tasting purposes (and the odd social gathering). Romina and I gave each other a leg up and got the key that was on top of the barrel (probably hidden for fear of intruders stealing our wines or maybe for discouraging little pests like us from getting plastered. And plastered we did get! We drank and drank, I played the trickster and my friend, to her convenience, happily showed her surprise as, yet another glass been filled. Even being caught by my uncle did not deter us from sneaking straight back in there and drinking some more.

A few hours later, well and truly legless, we heard a noise coming from the adjacent stables, my sister, returning from school, was coming through the back way. Drunk but well aware that she would take a lot of pleasure at getting us in trouble, we managed, somehow, to put the key back in its place and then we ran over to see her, displaying faces of sweet innocence. Unable to stand properly however, we held on to each other and faced my sister's eagled-eyed scrutiny. Unsurprisingly she immediately concluded that yes we had had a drink, plenty of drinks. We tried unsuccessfully to convince her that we were only pretending to be drunk but I believe the stink of booze on us gave us away. She marched over to the cellar with Romina and I following in tow, and to our horror, when she opened the door we saw a sight that we had not spotted during our session... the wine cellar floor was covered in puddles of wine.

My sister went straight upstairs to my mother, who by now wasn't shouting as the flooring had been dry for hours, and told her what we had done. Following a lot of blustering and shouting, there were two different outcomes to this experience. Romina, swayed all the way home, where her unsuspecting mother and grand-mother where making fresh ravioli. They only became aware of her condition, when they asked her to count them and mixing up all the numbers between one and a hundred, she managed to put holes in each and every one of the ravioli she touched. She was then put to bed and remained there sleeping for two days solid. I on the other hand at this early age did not take the easy root. Instead of sleeping the drunkenness off I went on to throw up for the following two days as I was on antibiotics for something or another and must have reacted badly to it, probably giving myself alcohol poisoning in the process.

This was the first of many alcohol related incidents that were to follow. Although, I wasn't a trouble causing child at all, on the contrary, I was always on my best behaviour and always (at least always strived to) conformed, with regards to the family's 'rules and regulations'. It was always about keeping the good old family reputation, that always was the, be all and end all in our household.

Luckily for me (or maybe not!) me drinking so much at times, especially from such a young age, was never an issue with my parents. In actual fact it was the cause for laughter and an excuse for another funny story to tell and maybe I, here and now, have my answer to my original question:

"What provoked my second memorable experience, my first drinking event?"

Answer: laughter, a feeling of recognition and existence, and much craved attention.

I don't remember doing much outside of working the farm as a family when I was little, although we were often hosts to gatherings and parties. The times we would go out altogether were few, generally to visit relatives otherwise the outings were split. For example, I don't remember going out with my sister at all but I remember being taken out by my uncle, together with Romina and her dad we would go to the cinema and watch old cowboy movies. Or at carnival times, Romina's family would take her and myself to some live local comedy shows for children where every kid would dress up as something or someone and wear beautiful masks. They were great shows and brought about a lot of laughter for us although at times, I did feel awkward that I was pretty much the only one there, who didn't have a costume.

With hindsight, maybe it was just as well that our outings as a family were very limited, because the car, was often a place where arguments would take place. From a young age I was already very sensitive and extremely aware of other people's feelings and pain (maybe a bit too much) so being in a confined place with nowhere to hide, it would choke me up inside having to listen to the grown-ups shouting and verbally hurting each other. Witnessing these powerful explosions of character through the eyes of a child, not being sure where or what started the outbursts, my stomach would churn, my body would tighten, watching, listening to my loved ones snatching pieces of dignity out of each other over what, certainly to me, were insignificant differences of opinion.

My visual memories of these outings have left me feeling throughout my life, and to an extent still feel and view as, sad and obscure; in a way, tainted.

Although the feuds were not limited to the trips, when they occurred at home, although painful, there, I had a way to escape them and busy myself. I would spend so much time trying to please, to be a mediator and restore peace trying to bring back smiles to those very faces that were shouting abuse and obscenities to one another (probably that is why now, my husband often tells me that I would be perfect for the UN peace ambassador position).

Having been apart from my family for most of my life, I know very little of my parents' background, but perhaps the little I know, may serve to give an insight into my parents' approach to parenthood how their walk of life, combined with the Italian culture, came to manifest their seemingly cold, strict ways.

Only the odd story I heard as a child and what bits of information transpire during odd conversations I have had with my sister, which, having been around them much more, can every so often provide a piece for my 'family puzzle'.

My father, a 5ft 7in stocky man, with a disarming smile and contrasting ice cold eyes. A child of the war, brought up through famine and working for a padrone (Boss) together with his family, in exchange for a home and a small share of the harvest as it was custom. In those days, as the son of a farmer, one of the 'lucky' few to get part of an education, 5 years in total. He lost his mum at a young age and (not to the same scale, but still traumatic) three fingers and a thumb to an agricultural machine while working on the land. His dream had always been to do away with 'il padrone', own his own land and his own house. Not long before marrying my mum he moved to the town where I would eventually be born. Contrary to my grandad's advice he took out a large loan to buy 14 hectares of land and the house that pretty much sat in the middle of it. Despite many of the arguments that took place, often as my grandad would express his fears and judgement toward such a bold step, accusing my dad of uprooting him, my new grandma and my uncle, for something that was destined to fail. My dad, however, never faltered. He worked hard, day and night to achieve his dream at the expense of family time and bonding. The pressure seemed to be always on. This also had a large impact on his relationship with my mum. Although my mum also worked the farm there were certain jobs that were a solo requirement, which would free my mum to 'socialise' alone with the neighbours. Alone in the fields and with a mind running wild my dad would become very jealous and take it out on my mum with accusations and insults often flying high.

My mum, a very naive and dependant woman. Similar upbringing to my dad as family social class goes but only had two years of education. After losing both her parents by the time she was eight, she was raised through what sounded like a harsh and abusive (through her recounts) aunty, until her elder brother became of age and took over till the time she married my dad. As a woman of that time she was never to have a mind of her own, totally dependent, always waiting for guidance with pretty much every aspect of life. However, being quite highly-strung, she did argue back when under accusation and that is when the arguments took a turn for the worst.

Again, around the age of five (Everything seems to have kicked off then), I was sent to stay with some relatives who lived about an hour away. The reason I was given for my little 'holiday', was that I was far too attached to the family and it was time to cut the apron strings. I was to stay there for a week of the summer. Now let me say, the relatives there, were lovely; my aunty, my grandad's sister was very loving and her children, all seven or eight of them, were all kind and trying to entertain me. The problem was, they were all grown ups, and for how hard they tried to keep me happy, their attempts fell like water off a duck's back. I was hurt, I didn't think I was "too attached" to anybody, I felt my place was at home with my family. Maybe, already from that age, as I know I did further on through my growing up years, I felt that I needed to have control, I needed to make sure that everybody was okay, that they were even 'safe' maybe. I was afraid that without me to keep an eye on the family, bad things would happen. I cried. Yes, I cried. Secretly as I didn't want to let my family down, especially my dad, who always promoted strength and keeping up the appearance of everything always been hunky dory to the rest of the world. However, I got caught out by a cousin that came to visit and told on me. My aunty, with her golden heart, made it so that my week-long stay was cut to five days and without getting me into trouble got my parents to pick me up.

During the same summer my sister went to the summer beach school where she stayed for two weeks. Being very different than myself, she loved being away from home and while I was at home, stressing and feeling that our family was falling apart, she was having a whale of a time. When she returned home I ran to meet her and checked that all was safe and well, with her beautiful smile and a glowing tan she produced a present that she had brought back for our mum. I followed behind as she climbed the stairs in to the house, when she lost her footing and the nice china basket gift she had, smashed in several pieces. My sister true to her personality, brushed herself up, said words to the sound of "oh what a shame" picked the pieces up and off she went to present my mother with her hand-glued present. On the other hand, I just froze I was devastated for her. Even then I had made it my responsibility, my situation to be resolved. I was upset for her, I embodied what, I believed, was her inner feeling. I suppose I know now that what I was doing was experiencing the moment as if it was I that had experienced it and mirrored the way I would have felt onto the person whose actions actually were; although probably their feelings couldn't have been more different than mine even if they had tried.

It is very clear to me now that I was already, at that young age, beginning to display signs of quite significant emotional issues and anxieties. But back then, within the culture and the life style, time and set up it went totally unnoticed, the family was far too busy and in a way, subject ignorant, to even pick up on the signs. Besides one of the most practiced attitudes beside that of screaming abuse at one another was one of 'if I don't know what to do about it I will ignore it'.

And with this principle in mind life carried on. Any advice was given in a life threatening manner and with such a rigidity that there was no room for even wrong thinking, never mind wrong doing.

Even from this age, five-six years old the messages were very serious and very grown up, they often followed conversations that someone that had come to the house had shared with my dad, or something that was heard on the radio or TV. Messages like "If you get pregnant before you get married I will kill you and your mother" and "Don't ever take sweets or anything from anybody, it could be drugs and then men will take advantage of you". Succeeding these statements were explanations delivered in no uncertain terms and left me very clear as to their meaning.

And for this, or in spite of this, as my young mind absorbed these beliefs and life instructions so directly imparted onto me, I worked even harder to impress, to be liked and accepted. Farm work, field work, and housework, whatever. Tending to any need my family might require, especially my father, I loved his praise and attention; I would feel so good and safe when my dad told me that I was such a good worker or when he played games with me pretending not to see me doing a job like helping him clear a room filled with seeds into another room. He would ask out loud "How have I managed to do such a big job so quick?" and show complete amazement mixed with a very pleased smile, when I would show myself and say "I helped you dad! It was me!"

Chapter Two – A Child's Pain

My first two years of school were spent in a little building in a nearby village. Again, I worked hard, it was very important that my reports were good, not only the written ones but also the verbal ones, those of the teachers, those of the people that lived near the school and could see me playing outside the building during lunch time, and those of the children that could go home and report to their parents about my behaviour. Small place and everyone knew my dad and everyone knew how to gossip. To be on the safe side, I was only friendly with the girls, thank God, Romina was there! Although this didn't at the time make things easier as she was a proper tomboy and loved joining in with the boys, playing and exchanging football cards. Because of the messages at home the mixing with the boys proved extremely difficult for me. The only boy I had really mixed with so far was my cousin Paolo who often came to visit at the house with my aunty, so when any other boy was paying me attention or God forbid say anything nice to me or about me, I used to slap them to make an example of them, encouraging anyone of the opposite sex to stay well clear of me.

I was well liked by teachers and second in class achievement; my cousin was top and this meant that at home the message remained that for how good I was, I was simply not good enough.

I can't quite remember if it was toward the end of the first year at school or the beginning of the second when young little me fell into the first depression. I remember feeling such an outsider, having to be so careful not to make mistakes and yet although I could control pretty much a lot of my world I could not control my mind, my thoughts. They would just slip in, unwanted and fought out, and yet they would just keep pushing their way in. Stupid little thoughts that would cause me to feel a guilt, an inner pain as if the silly images that were running through my mind had actually taken place. Silly or not these thoughts were not in agreement with the severe messages being given at home, they were rule breaking thoughts and if my dad knew… oh if my dad knew! I would be such a disappointing child.

"Must stop these thoughts…must stop the images…. No I don't like that boy; how could I fantasise he has given me a bracelet?! How bad of me… must stop the thoughts!" But the more I was trying to banish the thoughts the more they'd come, same ones, different ones, all filling me with guilt and pain, emotional and physical pain.

I began to cry, every day, gentle tears, heavy sobs, trying to keep the secret of these 'evil' thoughts. I stopped eating, I would just sit at the table and cry. To their credit my family did take notice of this and desperately tried to get me to tell them what was going on, even took me to the doctor, who had no idea what to do with me. Under the pressure of their questions and the heaviness of my heart, one by one all my 'secrets' started coming out of my mouth but the tears never stopped. It was not only the recent thoughts that were coming out, it was everything, everything that over my short life I had felt I could not share or I felt it was against the 'rules' but was sworn to secrecy; like by my sister for example (who by the way was totally unimpressed by what was going on and was threatening to kill me if I didn't keep my mouth shut about whatever little mischief she had been up to); the gates were open, every day something would come to me and the tears and the pain that accompanied them kept coming. What was astonishing, it was that, in my 'weakness' I was already showing my strength, as the person I chose to divulge to, out of everybody, was the very person that I thought was the hardest to please, the one that I was desperately trying to never let down, afraid that I could lose his love, the one that I constantly looked to for approval, the one that scared me the most, as his rejection would devastate me… my dad.

He tried to liven me up and laugh off my revelations but his worries began to show and it was through this time I got to see a different side of my dad. Meal times became a battle as I began to refuse to eat, not because I was attention seeking or I was being a brat, but simply because I couldn't. Even through the supplications of my father, begging me to eat, sometimes shouting out of desperation, or love, or both, I just sat there and cried. I remember one occasion my dad fighting with all his might his own tears, as he was watching his little girl wasting away and there was nothing he could do. This was one thing he could not control. My heart was hurting even more, the guilt became even more unbearable, I felt broken and now I was breaking my dad.

With time, when the tank become empty of any tears, I started to pick myself up and started to eat, play and my 'bad' thoughts lost their power and faded away.

Normal life resumed, working hard at school, doing jobs around the house, around the farm and in the fields. I still had to fight my demons, but after seeing the upset I had caused by showing my emotions I soon learned a new way, bottling things up. Of course it didn't always work I got caught shedding the odd tear but my God I made sure it was rare. I learned to deal with my dad's fierce stares, my mum's put downs and the watching the farm animals being killed and often having to help with the process.

What I couldn't deal with however, were my own 'mistakes', while I could justify and forgive anybody else's errors or less benevolent behaviours, I was very much less lenient on myself and my own learning lessons. Regardless of how good my intention was at the time, every action I took that didn't stand up to scrutiny, was to be added to the list of the "I hate me" campaign. I became very rigid with self-judgement; I really began to turn against me. Three incidents in particular dug deep within me and served to anchor my self-hate at this time. Events that ever since they took place, their memories have haunted me throughout my life. Although I now have the benefit and the ability to see the situation through the eyes of an adult, with a wider emotional understanding of myself and life, with the knowledge that we always do the best we can with the information we have at the time, I still recall these events with a deep sadness in my heart.

In my desperate attempts to please, find my power and at the same time save everything and everyone, I ended up killing (or at least being directly, yet accidentally responsible for the death) of three animals, a puppy, a kitten and a bird. Before anyone closes this book horrified at such revelations I am going to explain the circumstances and the mindset that caused these outcomes beginning with the puppy. My dad had put the latest litter of puppies on top of the open back of the three-wheeler vehicle my grandad used to get about, while he was roaming around the farm with the tractor. One of the puppies kept hanging over barking excitedly and all along almost falling. When I came by and saw this I was so afraid that he would fall and kill himself that I safely got him down, only to find out a short while later that my dad had put him there for his safety and because of my 'good deed' my dad had run him over.

The kitten was a different sense of guilt. I felt I did not do enough to save him. Although I felt I was the only one that fed him (there were a lot of cats around the farm and the family, not only were they trying to keep the breeding numbers down, they also weren't too bothered about the ones that had 'snuck through'), although I was there with him towards the end, every day with food and water. On a couple of occasions prior, when overwhelmed with the family dramas I had shut the door on him and shouted angrily. I felt terribly guilty and assumed his death was a result of my actions. The bird… Although a hunter, my dad on one occasion, brought home an injured bird. Despite my plea not to give it to me as I was afraid it would bite me, he told me to hold it while he would search for something to help it. Not wanting to disappoint and eager to save the bird's life I gave in. Still fearful of been hurt however, as the bird struggled to free itself I held his neck too tight and the inevitable happened. Distraught I ran to find my dad and although he was understanding and calm about it, I was crying and screaming. No words of reassurance on his part were any good…to me, I had just killed.

With my heart and mind being at such war with one another, each trying to make sense of everything, I can now 'see' and understand how these incidents were yet more nails in the coffin to any positive thought or opinion I had left of myself, as these actions only served to reinforce my beliefs of unworthiness and the feeling of being a really awful human being.

Chapter Three – Away From Home

Around the same time of me starting my first year at school my sister, five years older than me, following the Italian school system, was now doing her first year of secondary school and to do this she was sent to a convent school. My father got this idea from another local farmer that had sent his own daughter to this forsaken place.

This was devastating news for me because although the relationship I had with my sister wasn't the greatest, the very thing I was dreading was coming to life; my family was coming apart at the seams. Still, I soldiered on making the best of the times I would see her and kept my upset feelings to myself until to my total dismay, under the hat of "you are always suffering from tonsillitis and this place limits your winter exposure", two years later, at the age of eight, ready to begin my year three class, I was informed I was joining my sister and was sent to the convent school.

The school itself was small, six classrooms to accommodate students year one to eight (lower and upper school years). A good school, open to the local children too although not a first choice for many of the local families because of its location. Except for

RE which was taught by the half board local priest, all the other teachers were regular teachers, non-convent related, they came up to do their day work and went home. This part I liked. I also liked the scenery, the building was set very high up within the border of the centres Apennines Mountains in Italy. Clean fresh air, beautiful views absolutely stunning surroundings, these I can see and appreciate now, however, at the time it was the last thing on my mind as all this beauty only served to add to the heaviness of my heart and the tightening of my stomach as in the middle of this beauty and attached to the school, also joined by an inner passage (no doubt put there to save me from getting tonsillitis) was the bit I didn't like and what was going to be my home for the next six years of my life.

The boarding school was over an hours drive away from our home. Fighting back my tears and putting on the bravest face I knew, I said my goodbyes to my grand-dad, my uncle and to my mum, who seemed to behave as if shipping her daughter away from home was an everyday occurrence. Although I wonder, now that I am a mother myself and know the different hats that at times we have to wear as parents, whether her calm was a real state or whether she was hiding her emotions too. Still with my bag packed with very little clothes and a huge lump in my throat, one afternoon in mid-September 1977, I joined my sister in the car ready for my dad to take us there, the faraway place, the place that in my eyes was splitting my family up. We went a day early, so we could settle and be ready for the first day at school. Part of the building I was already familiar with as I had roamed around it on the times I had visited my sister. This time however, they looked different, they looked grey maybe to match the darkness I felt in my heart. Zoned out, I heard the nuns exchange pleasantries with my dad and after what seemed like no time at all, he was ready to leave. It was so hard saying bye to my dad as he was the last link I had right there, left with home.

The place was massive or at least that is what it seemed like to a young person of small stature.

There were so many rooms just on the ground floor, three huge staircases at different sides that took you to different parts of the building; one to the bedrooms, one to a raised outside enclosure and one that took to another massive dormitory that was no longer in use, except for when we put on our yearly stage play and concert, then we would use it as a base for changing. The room where I slept, at least the first year, was one of six, this one had a little outside balcony which was under no circumstances ever to be used.

Once shown to my dormitory where I rested my unpacked bag I was taken to the major common room to meet the rest of the girls. My sister jumped straight into it as she knew pretty much all of them from the previous year. Although I was a very sociable strong minded young lady, this pond I had just entered didn't feel right. Everything in me was screaming NO, NO, NOOOO!!

The first day at school in a new school it is always unnerving but my new teacher was really nice, half of the other pupils I already knew from the convent and the ones that came from the town, which also included boys, were a lively friendly bunch. School at least was looking like a good place to be.

I have to say the nuns were very pleasant at this time, then again of course they would be.

For the first few days they were very attentive and full of smiles (they did it with all the new girls) because this time was crucial, crucial to win me over, befriend me, as they knew that it is in the first few days, as the penny drops and the child realises mum and dad are not there at bed time, that they get home sick; and if mum and dad are a little soft (two years of having had my sister and these nuns had obviously learnt nothing about my parents), they could change their mind and take them home.

After all the boarding school was a business, they had to get as many places filled as they could, if the number of girls would drop too low, the boarding part would be shut down and the nuns would be relocated. As they had a nice little set up, this outcome is not something they would invite.

I was home sick even before I got in the car to leave home, but, determined as I was I was not going to let it show, and I didn't till the third day, on the way to school tears started flooding out, I sobbed and I sobbed. One of the nuns came out to see me, laughed it off and sent me to the classroom telling me I'll get over it, I remember the desperate attempt to stop my crying, to avoid being 'an embarrassment', struggling to hold on to my pride and struggling to breathe through the heavy tears I composed myself and vowed to myself that no tear would leave my eyes again for any of them to see.

There was a firm regime in place from the moment we got up to the time we went to bed, and no one was to stray from it. The rules as I found out as time went by, were very clear and very simple; even though they came as a shock and a sharp reality to a free spirited, highly strung farm girl like me.

The nuns were now your 'parents', they were to be treated as such and as such, held all parental powers. BUT, you could only address them formally, as you would a stranger, no closeness to be established, they were the system. You were not to have a personality of your own or say or do anything without asking permission; you would be chastised, put in a corner and shamed in front of everyone and sent to confession where the priest would punish you some more. You were not to have an opinion or, God forbid, contradict or question anything the nuns said. You were to be weighed within the first few days of arrival and you would be fattened up so they could prove to your parents they were getting good value for money. You were to sit like a lady, no slouching and certainly no elbows on the table; a nun would circle the tables with a needle in her hand to prick anyone that didn't do it properly. Like it or not, you would eat everything you were given, if you happened to have a stomach bug and be sick thus throw up their food like I did ONCE you were screamed at and again, be made an example of. You were to go to the chapel, also part of the building twice a day as a unit, once for prayers and once for mass. You were to study hard in school and for several hours out of school. Only top results were acceptable. Cleaning had to be thorough in the morning, before school, all bedrooms, bathrooms, dining room and common rooms all clean and sparkling; after lunch and dinner all washing up were to be done and kitchen and dining all restored to full hygiene. We were to wash properly every day but shower once a week. Although showers were individually enclosed, they had to be taken with your pants on because you couldn't be fully naked even to your own eyes (still today I can sometimes struggle to feel at ease showering naked). You were not to have a best friend or at least be seen to spend too much time talking to one person separate from the mass on more than two days in a row. Nothing was private not even your mail, any letter would be opened and given to you only if deemed 'respectable', if in the nuns' eyes they contained any inappropriate words or content YOU, the recipient would be held responsible and as such punished. You were to say prayers out loud with the rest of your room-mates as soon as you went to bed and the lights were out, if you didn't say them properly you were made to get up and made to stand in the middle of the corridor bear footed, cold and to serve yet again, as an example to the others. After prayers one of the nuns would pace up and down the dormitory and the corridor to ensure silence and good behaviour which to my total confusion included sleeping with both your hands on the pillow, under your head because good girls, apparently can't warm them up between their knees!

I have to say over the years I got into trouble a lot, everything seemed to be my fault. Two things in particular didn't help; one - that I always stood up for what I thought was right for me and others, especially if I saw someone been bullied, upset, or unfairly treated. Even then, I was all about happiness for all and saving the world. Two - I was the daughter of a communist and the nuns knew this, as my dad always made sure people knew his political stance. I grew up with the face of Stalin the Russian communist political leader hung on our dining room wall!

As the nuns were well educated, they knew full well that communism is of atheist nature thus does not recognise God (and there is me, daughter of an avid communist, in a convent school where pretty much EVERYTHING is about God and praying to Him). Although the nuns never made direct remarks about the family's political view, there were many related digs made when I was being scolded for whatever thing I was been accused of at the time. Let's put it this way, if something was missing, if someone spilled something, if a boy said he liked me it was my fault. Whatever the argument, whatever the reasons, people or situation, it was always me in the confession box.

It was pointless of me running to mum and dad with any complaints as I soon realised that despite the difference in political views and backgrounds both parties, parents and nuns, stood together in their beliefs of strict upbringing, a child does not have a voice and needs to be shaped through rigid discipline including bullying, emotional blackmail and all sorts of scare tactics. Words to the sound of "You are going to hell" (with the full description of the hell I would find myself in, without skipping the purgatory bit) and "The world is coming to an end and we are all going to die very soon" are totally terrifying to an eight, nine-year-old girl away from her home.

Soon broken, submissive with my head bowed down, a shadow of my former confident self, there I learned to 'act' a life, practicing to be someone else. I remember one of the nuns commenting with a look of contempt, "she always behaves as if someone is watching her". And with that practice, I slowly or maybe quickly, forgot ME.

Even though the convent life swiftly became the norm, it was not without the lack of the pungent gut pains and the knots in my throat that I got the moment I woke in the morning once I realised where I was.

Parents were allowed to come and visit every Sunday afternoons and most of them did. My parents however, decided that the distance to travel was a bit too far and for that, every other week would be more than reasonable. Eventually the 'every other week turned into every three weeks and then once a month especially in the winter time. We were not allowed to go and greet our parents even though we could see them arriving, we would have to wait until called and escorted to meet them by the nuns which again at those times were all full of smiles and warmth.

One thing that did stick with me, was when the other girls' parents came, they would sit with their child in a corner or in a place somewhere where they could have some quality time, cuddles and private chats. When mine came, they would first spend time talking to the nuns, exchanging looks of commiserations and making derisory comments if there had been an event where the nuns felt I had messed up on; then, they would sit with me, somewhere where they could also chat to the other girls there, making it a social gathering. They would spend a couple of hours and then leave. Although the time I had with them wasn't the closest or the warmest, I felt so empty when they left, so unsettled, anxious, restless and sad all at once. Again I felt it in my stomach but mainly it grabbed my throat. Following this pattern of somatic manifestation, it's no wonder that eventually, in my older years, I ended up getting my tonsils out and developing a stomach ulcer. Feelings of being in a prison where time goes very slowly, powerless in making any changes. These feelings got so engrained within me over this time, that occasionally they still show themselves, now, after all these years, on late Sunday afternoons early evening when I am not engaged or engrossed in something, they show their ugly heads.

We would go home four times throughout the year, the first break was two days in the autumn, the 31st of October and the 1st of November, the day of the dead and All Saints' Day respectively. These two days I would spend together with my family going around all the various cemeteries where the 'closest' relatives (three generation prior and 4th cousins removed) were buried.

The second break were the Christmas holidays which were generally a couple of weeks long, these I would really look forward to as it was a tradition in Italy that Christmas is that one day of the year which is to be spent with your immediate family nucleus, and although there were no presents really, for me the fact that I had the family all together again was a present in itself. There were times however that my parents did leave me wondering whether they were coming to get me and take me home for this long awaited holiday, as they would leave it to the evening to come and pick me up, when everyone else had gone home and I would be at evening mass all by myself with the nuns and the locals with no phone call to let me know what was happening, fighting the tears and the feeling of loneliness and abandonment yet again. On the plus side they always came even if they had to send my uncle as my dad was still busy, doing what, I'm not entirely sure as a farmer's work is very limited in the winter, but non the less busy.

Although Christmas could go either way, pleasant and peaceful or strained and argumentative, I would cherish this time with my family and going back to the convent after this holiday was heart breaking.

This holiday and the summer holidays were the hardest to go back from, this one probably because of the holy festivity itself plus my birthday would soon follow but by then I would already be back in school; the summer one, because by the time I had to return, I would have spent three months fitting back in with the, although troubled, very much loved home routine and creating more golden memories with my dearest friend Romina.

The trips back to the convent school, that road, every bit of scenery my eyes rested upon during that drive returning me to that building and its inhabitants (the nuns) would cause my stomach to churn, a sinking feeling that required the gathering of all of my resources to stop the tears from running fearful yet again, of being a disappointment to my dad, the disappointment I so dreaded to be.

The third visit home would be for the Easter holidays. This holiday would only be a week, maybe at a push, 10 days long. Although I was happy to go home, this holiday didn't fill me with excitement like the Christmas and the summer ones. Not sure why, maybe because it wasn't a very long holiday and also this festivity wasn't 'felt' at our home and as a general local culture, as special as the Christmas season. It would not carry the family closeness that Christmas brought. While the latter was a close family affair, for Easter anyone was welcome to visit and living in a house on the top of a hill in the beautiful countryside not many friends and family relatives would miss the opportunity to spend a day in the lovely crisp air. Don't get me wrong, it's not that I didn't like the company or the 'parties' but yet again I became a 'tool' in a tense household where my dad would demand that everything and everyone was and looked perfect to anyone in the outside world. Anything that he conceived to be not good enough, was met with an icy dirty look hidden, of course, from the guest that were instead met with grand smiles and loving welcoming gestures. Once met by one of the 'icy stares' yourself or catching mum at the end of one, you knew that more than likely, when the guests would leave, there would be fireworks and not of the nice type. This would give me that fight or fly feeling, that walking on egg shells sensation, that need of pleasing and appeasing my father, desperately checking within his eyes for a smile, for a sign that all was well. Whether I found that smile or not often the fireworks did ignite anyway. The shouting and the verbal abuse between mum and dad, the finger pointing and the occasional slap my mum would receive, were often how these jolly meant occasions were rounded up. Needless to say the feelings these would leave within me were soul destroying and I would be left to wonder which was the better of the two evils. Despite of it all, home always won over the convent school. I just had to work harder, be a better girl, a really good girl. Be extra nice to everyone, brighten up and water down any possible flammable situation and smooth over all the cracks.... The fourth home coming was the summer holidays. These were the best and so long awaited. A good three months home, which, although it still came with the jobs of keeping the family glued and the farm going, I welcomed.

The first couple of days would be spent getting reacquainted with my home surroundings after that a new 'normality' would resume.

Everyone had to contribute to the household, no one was 'being carried' regardless of age or gender. If you could carry the weight the job was yours. No choice.

I would be given instructions and be shown what food, food mixture I was to give to the different animals around the farm, what container was used for what, how much to each and how to clean each animals living area. This had to be done every morning and evening.

And then there were the other jobs, keeping the house clean and doing the laundry. With no washing machine, every item of clothes had to be hand washed, this task took place on a cement basin attached to the well I took the water out of for the animals. So, armed with washing powder or a bar of special soap designed for clothes, and a battery operated radio for entertainment, pretty much on a daily basis, I would become the laundry master.

Who would have said in those days that one day I would be in England not wanting to have much to do at all with anything Italian! While then as a child, while doing the clothes washing, I disliked and opposed listening to any of the radio's stations, that played any English and American tunes, I only listened and sang along to Italian music and would get really cross on those occasions when my sister would join me with the laundry and insisted on listening to foreign music radio stations. If anyone were to bet then, which of the two would be the one flying the nest, turning on her heels and walking away from it all, they certainly would not have picked me!

The day would start very early, 7 o'clock at the latest I would have to be up and ready to start the chores. If I failed to be up by that time and my parents, normally my mum was back from whatever place she had gone to work that day, together with my dad, usually at one of our fields or neighbouring farms, and catch me still in bed, I would be in big trouble. I would be shouted at, pinched or leg slapped; so oversleeping wasn't a good idea. Maybe that is why now I am so overly careful with setting up alarm clocks, often doubling up on them, and with general time keeping not only for me but for my family also, I tend to drive my children crazy with timing and punctuality. Still, when all the jobs were done and my parents were working away and I wasn't required to help in the fields I would be free to play with my friend Romina, who again, would have to come to me because I was not allowed to leave the house. These play times were wonderful, although they could be troubled by the odd falling out or spat especially if my sister was involved, they were so free from any of the pressure, judgement and constant rules I was so accustomed to.

Many were the lessons and skills learned during my younger years, all of them, as life naturally developed, very useful and indispensable in my adulthood (although maybe some of them definitely more emotional than practical!) but, like many children, I didn't realise it at the time.

I didn't, and still don't, begrudge the learning, not even one lesson as I wouldn't be me in all my colours and shades now without each and every one of them. Although I have to admit, the manner and the harshness in which some of these were taught, I did begrudge a little during my emotional enlightenment.

Many and varied were the practical experiences, during my childhood which my parents thought would make a good wife out of me. These included all imaginable household's jobs, caring for the farm animals and then help with their slaughter, learning to drive tractors, seed sowing in the fields, harvesting all

sorts of crops, making wine, making fresh pasta, salami and sausages, and other more original jobs like making cartridges for the firearms my dad and uncle used for hunting and the one I am about to describe.
In our household even from a young age nothing was given for free everything had to be earned. I remember earning my very first watch by guarding onion seeds from ants. Massive plastic sheets packed with harvested onion seeds were laid out on one of our fields so they could dry in the sun. I had to spend my day walking around the sheets and raising the borders so that the ants that were coming to steal the seeds would fall back inside and in so doing maximising income for the harvest.

The emotional lessons were a 'solo' learning experience. Scars I picked up along the way as my responses to any event or situation were left unguided and unexplained; left my little busy mind to put things together in an ambiance where anger was easily fuelled and where, I felt, there was no space for errors. Although indispensable to my later life, this part of learning for me, so much a fighter but a very sensitive soul, was what gave birth to the unrest within me. The need to 'go deeper' and look for the meaning of everything, the wanting to change the world, contrasting the embedded feeling of having to hold back because of how small and insignificant I felt I was. The sadness and the frustrations at the pain, the anger, at times the hate, I 'saw' in my loved one's eyes, were a huge contradiction to the loving world I desperately looked to bring to life. Within and without, I felt my life was full of colossal opposites. All of this brought about a profound confusion, creating an emotional storm an inner conflict at my core. The learning that no matter what I did, was never good enough, over time, formed a belief of nullity, a huge feeling of unworthiness. The words that years later I related to my counsellor and still resonate clearly in my mind, are the words of my mum saying to me "I wish I had given birth to a bunch of thorns rather than having had you" (and this just for not having set up the rabbits' hatch to her standard). Those very words, as well as more of the kind, were to forge an intense innermost discord allowing for more and more insecurities to creep up and self-beliefs to slowly and steadily plummet. Still, the world was not going to see my 'weakness', my pain, and with a smile of my face I marched on.

Over these years the feeling of not belonging began to grow and strengthen with every new situation I was faced with. Times like playing volleyball on a Sunday afternoon with the local children really brought it home. This was my home village, the place where every child and every adult knew one another so well and yet, there was me, except for Romina I really didn't 'know' anybody. Of course, I knew their names, their family names, but there was no comfort, no closeness like there were between the other children.

They all knew each other so well. Although shy, already uncomfortable with my image, as anxious as one could be, by Romina's side I stood; on several non-raining summer Sunday afternoons, chatting, playing, acting like I was the most confident person on this planet, like butter would not melt in my mouth and all along, inside, struggling to breath for fear that someone would 'see' right through me and my insignificance. On the other end, the convent school, although it had all the requisite to feel like a home, being the constant, the invariable, the stable and predictable, deep inside it never ever was home. I felt a stranger within my family, a stranger within the social circle, a lodger, not too much of a welcomed guest at the convent school. And life would have it even today although very comfortable and at home with myself, my home, and my surroundings after living in a different country for 26 years I am considered and seen as foreign, a 'non be-longer' in both countries, Italy and England equally. This makes me chuckle, as now, after many years, those feelings of non-belonging have changed into feeling of uniqueness and this makes me feel special (at least most of the time).

It is amazing how feeling the odd one out, at various stages of your life can mean a totally different thing. Through the learning and the growing, changing and moulding, the mind opens and creates different perceptions. While as a child I perceived this to be a negative state, a state of loneliness and isolation, now as an adult, I perceive it as a positive. I am now grateful for it, as I look at it with a sense of achievement, a sense of power, a sense of having outgrown certain people and situations, I take it as sign, that I have reached yet another level of understanding and that a new level of growth and learning is at my disposal. I now believe that, 'feeling left out' is actually the inner part of me saying "this is not who I am anymore, I have raised my game".

Chapter Four – "Misfit"

With my exceedingly high grades under my belt, the next unequivocal step would be 5years of college studies followed by university as it is the customary educational route in Italy. With such a report I could choose any subject, any school, and any direction but my intentions were very different and despite the suggestion and recommendation and high expectations of every teacher in the school I chose a completely different path. By this point I had an inner desire to escape, to get away from all that surrounded me, not so much to run from my problems, from my unrest, although maybe this also played a part, but because I 'felt' I was to follow a different path. I felt I didn't belong there, that there was a different life awaiting me, not there, not in 'that world'. So, I decided that the study and career would have to wait and that my ticket to 'different' was going to be catering. You can be a waitress pretty much anywhere in the world and earn enough to begin a new life, the life I 'felt'. With this in mind, the local professional school of catering is where I went to, which (bonus!), delighted my dad as I would be learning languages (his dream) and I would save him a fortune in school fees. Although much closer to home this school was also a boarding school, it was to last only 2 years and would provide me with the qualifications I needed. At this time, I wasn't thinking very big, certainly not moving to live permanently in a different country, no. I was just looking at being away for seasonal work, being away summers and winters, maybe on the coasts of Italy or maybe the Suisse Alps or the French Massifs. I certainly, by now could not envisage a life at home anymore, in fact due to the many inner battles caused by the constant feeling of not belonging, I already could not feel my home of origin as my home anymore. This filled me with sadness and a deep sense of loneliness which again would bring about, over my mid teenage years, more bouts of depression, some much deeper and more self-destructive than others.

The school was based at a 4-star hotel. I remembered being dropped off by my father, I was absolutely petrified as I watched him drive away and I stood with my bag of clothes in my hands, left to find out where I was going, between one smile and a 'hello' trying to find where I needed to be, praying and wishing all along to be invisible.

After meeting with an allocated staff member, being given time tables and a quick run through of the run of things we were sent to our rooms and put our stuff away.

The boys' accommodation was spread over two floors on much more humble settings. Us girls, because of a much lower number, were given the top floor of the hotel, the same rooms as the hotel clientele and following my previous accommodation and life style of the convent school, this was a great surprise, plus, having found out that one of my better friends from there, had also come to this place, made for a seemingly good start.

Little did I know at this point that this school was going to present me with new, very different challenges; not academic, although performance was effected, but emotional, personal, and interpersonal challenges. One hundred and twenty boys and nineteen girls, a massive change to the convent school. Here is where the discovery of relationships between boys and girls took place, where I came to have my first boyfriend, where I developed and enforced my discomfort of being looked at, at being at the centre of attention, especially by the male population. Where I began my battle with food, weight and the all general image issues.

At first I was like a wildcat hitting everybody that slightly touched me. I was struggling to cope with the number of boys that were around, I was unsure on how to behave around them, at first all it took was for one of them to touch me on the shoulder and say good morning and I would slap them right across the face.

Then I began to study the interaction between the other girls and boys noticing how they laughed, played, mess around with one another, and those that formed relationships, comfortably hugged and kissed in front of everybody, totally unashamed, unembarrassed even when the prefects reprimanded them.

For somebody as shy as I was, the requirements and set ups of the school were quite demanding. Beside the actual study lessons that covered a mixture of subjects, including a variety of languages and etiquette; we also had the practical aspect. For those like myself that had chosen waitressing, this involved serving meals in weekly rotation between the hotel 1st class restaurant, where you served the hotel clientele; and the canteen, where you served the other students whilst still keeping all the mannerisms and perfectionism of the service that one would expect in the hotel restaurant.

Although I found it petrifying and very unnerving working in the actual restaurant, for me, it was easier than working in the canteen where I felt I was on show in front of my peers and that was where I felt exposed and at my weakest. What didn't help was that I felt… no, I believed I was so much less than every other girl there. I believed I wasn't as pretty, as thin, as charming, as friendly as them. I believed that I didn't have an inch on their massive personalities, smooth ways, their sexy walks and fancy short skirts. I have to say my wardrobe wasn't the best, to add to my shame, even my uniform which consisted of white blouse and black skirt looked like I borrowed it from a purist middle aged woman compared to my fellow pupils lovely fitted ones. No matter how many advances I had to turn down or how many boys I had to slap for saying they like me I never believed that I was good enough, that anybody could ever like anything of me. Despite the other girls telling me they noticed how certain boys looked at me, how their behaviour around me suggested they liked me, how the presents I received from some of the boys on my birthday were an indication that they liked me a little more than just as a friend, I was totally oblivious to all of these messages, after all, how could it be? I simply wasn't lovable. I wasn't good enough.

Soon another issue emerged. While I was in the canteen during a lunch sitting, as part of the group whose turn it was to be served, I began to furtively look around at the other tables, the boys' tables, and if I spotted anybody looking at me munching away, that was my cue, I would stop eating. That was the beginning of my battle with food. Right there I developed an adversity to food, a very uncomfortable relationship with eating and even more so eating while being watched.

Even though with time some of my behaviour around

boys mellowed my self-conscious behaviour worsened. I became very rigid in my approach to most things and always strived for perfection which brought me to question and 'watch' myself and my surroundings all of the time. As perfection is an unattainable goal, my insecurities grew and the few good aspects I still liked about me, like being a top class student and (the belief of) being the responsible, good, obedient, respectable girl, soon crumbled, and the girl I felt I knew and I had been trained to be, quickly vanished.

With so many themes to deal with, so many aspects of my life that I felt I was unequipped for, with so many things to learn about, to accept, and come to terms with, so many beliefs and new situations to tend to… it felt like I was constantly swimming to keep my head above water and yet spectacularly drowning at the same time. Yet again, however, the world was not to know or see any of it, it would not know of my tiredness and of my struggles. Head up high, smile on face, laughing if others laughed (even if I didn't get the jokes), walking as others did and eventually, smoking and getting into amorous relationships as the rest of my peers did.

To add to my shame and future guilt, seeing that, as per usual, I never fancied anybody, I trusted the 'taste' of my good friend from the convent school. In so doing, I fooled around with one of the older boys she liked, and although he had no interest in her, to my horror and a lesson quick learned at that innocent age, it almost cost me our friendship.

My first kiss however, was to be shared with none other than the nephew of the most vicious of the convent's nuns, who, to my amazement had fancied me from when he met me at the convent school and fancied me still! One day he contacted me and we decided to meet. My innocent self, swiftly fell for all the beautiful words he spoke, just to mention one and to give you an idea of my total innocence, the following was one of his sentences to me. The following is a literal translation: - "When you descended the bus and I saw you, it was like I was watching The Madonna, beautiful, right there before me" No more words are needed to describe my gullibility.

We met up a few times, hardly ever in town, as I wasn't allowed to go and if any of my father's many friends and acquaintances saw me I would certainly be in a world of trouble. He mainly came up to the hotel school gardens and nearby bar, and there is where I started to become acquainted with all my insecurities, my fears, my guilt and my demons. Even the act of laughing and rolling around the grass with him took on a meaning of sin and guilt within me. If for any reason the rolling would stop with him on top of me the guilt and anguish would sit with me for days, consuming me, spreading such a bitter taste in my conscience that would eat me up from the inside out. I was a sinner, a bad girl, a disgrace to the family name. What if my dad, my mum, found out that their daughter had behaved in such a 'sluttish', disreputable, dishonourable manner...?! The guilt would eat me up after any new discovery or questionable behaviour (questionable by me), it would build, it would choke me. I found refuge and comfort in confiding to a lady that worked in the hotel kitchen. At the end of the restaurant shift when on duty, during the washing and cleaning I would look for the opportunity to speak to this wonderful warm kind lady; she took her time talking to me and reassuring me that I wasn't Satan's daughter and that my experiences and interactions, were nothing but normal for a girl of my age and that I should relax and enjoy my beautiful young years. However, although temporarily appeased by her calm and positive reassurance, my conscience would soon proceed to giving me a good kicking back 'home'; back 'home', to doubts, inner battles and general bad feelings about myself.

Needless to say, due to my stiff attitude and approach to anything to do with the relationship, ingrained fears and the unwillingness to take the relationship even half a step forward, the nun's nephew got quickly bored and all of a sudden stopped coming to seeing me or keeping any contact.

By the end of my first year, although I had created a controlled environment, everyone pretty much knew where they stood with me; so, except for the few 'hard of hearing', which I still beat up, and although still very self-aware, I had allowed or shall I say, had pushed myself to experiment more of a 'normal' life. I tried smoking which although unable to do properly, and choked every time I put a cigarette in my mouth, I mastered the practice of 'pretending'. It is a fact however that whether able or unable to be a true smoker I kept this habit for many years. In fact, despite being a very poor liar and being rubbish at any form of deceit, as I always got sussed out every time I tried, I was able to keep it from my parents until I was in my thirties (the fact that I lived away from home for most of these years, I admit, did help).

I also tried to be more flirtatious but most of the time felt very uncomfortable and very much a fool. As my convent friend had chosen different courses than I she had bonded and spent more time with another girl, I became more lonely and panicky. I tried desperately to fit in with the other girls but felt I was so different. I started to attention seek, playing for drama, playing the shock card, the melodramas, in order to be liked and accepted, by the people in my group as well as desperately trying to hold on to the safety and comfort of my old friendship and the group she comfortably, confidently had adapted to. I was jealous of my friend's ability to break free from all the rules, the rigid beliefs we had conformed to during those years in the convent school. Of course at that age and being in the situation, I didn't have the understanding that I can now draw upon. I didn't take into consideration how much more open minded and relaxed a family she had, her mum was her best friend! (My mum? I had not a resemblance of a close relationship with); I had 6 years of indoctrination at the school, she barely had 2. Still, none of this entered my mind, I could only see her successes, her happiness and her glee in contrast to my failures, my image as a misfit and insignificance. New traits of comparison that I would frequently use in years to come. Instead of using her ability to fly as a lesson to learn, I studied it and used it to beat myself up.

To add to it none of my melodramatic attention seeking behaviour never really worked and I grew to be less and less confident, more lonely and my self-worth plummeted to a new level of low.

Every weekend we got to go home, for me home to a family of strangers, tension and work and an emptiness inside that I didn't know how to fill. By the time the first school summer holiday came I had another major break down.

Chapter Five – I Hate Me

On completing my first year at the school, although not my best ever results, I was, as always recognised, as the most sensible, responsible and trusted student; and therefore, was immediately offered a place to work at the restaurant for the summer season which of course I happily accepted. As it was the summer holidays however, as well as spending my days off at home, I was expected by my family to also make my way home as often as possible in between my working hours (using my moped). This was partly to keep me away from 'trouble' and mostly to get me to help out at the farm. The days and time spent at the hotel working were more bearable as I was engaged and focussed on my job and interacted with the customers. This meant I had less time to live in my head and dwell on my thoughts, and the 'darkness' that squeezed my soul. The times at home however were a different matter. Here is where, left to my untamed self, I would lose all self-imposed restrictions and undress the mask I showed the world. Here is where I came back to the raw, naked me. In these lonely moments, I would cry tears from my deepest self, I would release so much self-hate, smack my face, pinch myself, pull hair out of my head and, often, looking in the mirror, I would call myself the most awful degrading insulting names my mind could muster.

My dad noticed that something was not right with me, in his eyes, I was not looking well and my eating habits weren't satisfactory. He marched me down to a doctor at the hospital, friend of his, to put me right. After a few questions and engaging my evasive glances a couple of times I guessed that he read me pretty well. He had obviously realised that there was not a chance on the planet I would say a word of what I was going through in front of my dad. He quickly told my dad not to worry too much, he explained how it can be hard for young people at times in this changing world but that he would be there for me to have a chat whenever I wanted. Holding my eyes, he insistently reiterated to me to just go and see him, no need to call ahead just turn up and ask to see him. I remember it so clearly in my mind, the very next time I had one of my self-hate episodes, with tears streaming down my face barely able to see the road, I rode my moped at maximum speed to the hospital to take him up on his kind, insightful offer. Holding a blink of hope in my heart that this doctor might have some answers to rid my pain, a silent expectation that he might hold the key to my inner comfort, some crumbs of inner peace…but when I got to his office and asked his secretary to see him, I was met with a "Sorry the doctor is not in today". I never went back.

I carried on plodding along, acting, and showing very little of my pain to my family, and absolutely nothing to the rest of the world. I worked hard at the hotel, as well as at home and complied with all that was required of me at both ends. At a spa near the hotel there was a disco at night at weekends, which, despite my parents' displeasure, I snuck to and while there I fought to fit in to the best of my ability. I observed other young people having fun, their interactions and alcohol fuelled laughter. This was a major contrast to the weekends I was at home and went with my mother to the local ball room dancing. Two worlds apart and I, a girl with no identity, was stealing a bit of both, trying to feel, to work out where I best belonged.

Before long the school resumed and this time I took a different approach. I decided that I was now more experienced and thus more 'qualified' to behave more grown up. I wasn't so harsh on the boys, I allowed myself to mix more with them and together with my convent school friend I started to take on 'full time' smoking, take more excursions to town and wear borrowed miniskirts. Despite all this theatrical behaviour on the surface underneath I followed my original pattern which brought about decision and outcomes that caused even more self-damage. An example of this was my choice of boyfriend. As I already mentioned I did not lack the attention of the opposite sex and I could have taken my pick, and with hindsight, there were some really lovely boys. However, with my mindset levelled at low frequency energy, I opted for the boy that 'I felt sorry for'. I opted for the one that I thought the teacher didn't like much, the one I felt the adults were treating too harshly the one with the scar on his chin, the one that maybe wasn't' the most handsome but although a bit of a rebel, I thought looked sad when being reprimanded. Without any thought that there might have been a good reason for him being scolded, I decided I was going to be there for this guy. Anyway this boy, which I shall call Roberto, became my boyfriend and I was to stay with him for the next three years. The relationship was very turbulent and controversial. Turbulent because we were both very insecure and therefore very jealous of one another and also because he came from a different background than mine. His was much more free spirited, he was a city boy free to come and go as he pleased, the family had a bit of money and he was used to getting his way a lot. Controversial at school, because a lot of the teachers that had become aware of our relationship were not best pleased as, like I said, they did not view him as a good character while I was the good amenable girl that he might just wreck. Controversial at home because my mum wanted me to be with a boy that she liked from the ballroom dancing and this one in her eyes, as my mum has always been about looks and appearance, was not good looking enough for me, so she turned against him from moment go.

The only way for us to see each other was by him coming to my house, as I was not allowed to go out just in case people saw us and put two and two together and made twenty-five. This would have meant guaranteed gossip coming my way and that was not an option. At the end of the second year some students were put in touch with hotels from the seaside coast for summer jobs, and those who weren't, pupils like Roberto, had to find their own work placement. One of the other girls, Elisa, and I were put in touch with a lovely lady that had a place near Rimini and she came to meet us at the school and offered us a summer job there and then. At this point I was encouraged at home to make my own decisions with regards to my life. I had to show I was ready to fly the nest. No matter how small or big the decision, it had to pass the good side of 'what are people going to say?' regardless if it was good for me or not or whether it was something that made me happy or not. The only thing that would override this question was if there was money to be made and take home, then, it was always a good decision. All the same, I was more often than not told "no, you have made the wrong choice, call them back and tell them…" despite of how much embarrassment it might cause me. On other occasions, where I wasn't told to call back and cancel, my parents made a point of making me go, ridden with guilt as they would emphasize how bad the choice was, still refusing to allow me to change the plan. One occasion I recall in particular, I was asked by Roberto to go with him to an interview for a job near the hotel I was about to go and work at in the summer (2 hours' drive from my house) I asked my dad if it was ok, he told me "you are old enough to make decisions like this" I picked up the phone told my Roberto that I would love to go, thinking that was a nice thing to do, go and support him and at the same time I would have the opportunity to see where I was going to work. From the moment I put the phone down I was chastised for making such a poor choice. I was told that I would now HAVE TO go but…" what are people going to say?!" followed by a lot of head shakes and displeased looks. This did not improve my confidence and self-esteem and might explain, to the despair of friends, partners, colleagues and acquaintances, why throughout my life I have never been very good at making decisions and played the passive role when one has had to be made.

As it all panned out the following summer I did go to work at that holiday resort and so did Roberto. I was now sixteen and I was to spend three months away from home, again having to adjust to, live, and sleep in a new place with new rules and new people, this time mainly with adults. Although I had Elisa there to share a room and work with, and this could have been of comfort, we weren't exactly close. In fact, this proved to be one of the challenges I encountered, as she was quite manipulative, moody and had a thirst for power and control, which was the perfect ailment for my well-developed need for pleasing and my deep-rooted fear of not being liked or accepted. These two bittersweet companions of mine came out to dance like it was the party of the century. It is so true that we attract people and situations that serve to prove and reinforce our inner most common thoughts, emotions and that which we come to believe! It is such a throw off that we automatically use such techniques to prove ourselves right, to reassure ourselves that we know ourselves, that our beliefs are true, that more often than not, as a lot of us are more responsive to negative feeds, we end up 'proving', we go out of our way to convince ourselves, that we are unworthy, meaningless and full of negative traits.

This time away served me to feel even more estranged from everyone as well as from myself. I felt myself getting more and more lost as I felt I was stepping even further away from past imparted rules and moving into new forbidden territories. Even though I was still following the main protocol - I was working hard, I was very much liked, trusted and respected by the hotel owner; as well as feeding my demons of insecurities - I was constantly bowing down to Elisa my 'on pedestal' school 'friend' asking for the hundredth time why did she stop talking to me? And when told "I shouldn't need to tell you, you should know", asking forgiveness for whatever I did that could have upset her so much. Even the complying to my father's demand of "don't touch the wages", "bring all the money home", "only use the minimal and indispensable for minor treats, you are there to work not to have fun", didn't help me with feeling grounded. Following these familiar patterns was no longer a deterrent to my falling even more into the hands of my self-destruction. Although Roberto had no issues with money and was happy to pay for extra treats for both of us, my guilt grew every time I went out as I felt I was disobeying my father. It was also during this time that my sister had her second child and although I went to visit her and baby at the hospital (a demand from my father as yet again, the family were to show this great unity to the world), I felt very disconnected, very detached and estranged to the family. I felt as if I was visiting extended relatives. Despite all of these disturbing feelings and emotions, the major thing that caused me to feel I had stepped into a place of no return, a place of extended self-hate, a place where I had considered the most dangerous of them all, a place of disgrace and betrayal (toward my father), I had my first sexual experience. Needless to say it was nothing to write home about (for more reason than one!) as my reasoning for taking such a step, ironically, were the outcome of lessons, beliefs resulting from my dad's teachings- the need to please, not to let down, as well as the fear of losing my boyfriend, the only person I thought I really 'had' and cared about me then. In taking such a step however, I opened a can of worms much bigger than I even knew. Beside the excess fear of pregnancy, of death, of myself and my mother as my father had often threatened, it felt wrong to me. Although I didn't know it then, I wasn't in love and the act itself was done out of duty, out of giving in to my boyfriend's insistence, for fear of losing him. Done for the need to hold on, without sentiment or personal intention, it destroyed even more of me, who ever that me was, as I didn't know her, the girl within…yet, I felt I had truly betrayed her and the deed could not be undone. Still, although I prayed every night, petrified to my core, for me not to get pregnant, yet expecting this God that the nuns had me believing, unforgiving and vengeful to punish me, "The show must go on" attitude was introduced once more. The need to keep my outer world afloat was deemed, once again, more important than this sensitive inner girl that I didn't even know, and more water was added to the vase that eventually would spill over.

I floated through that summer job only to return home empty hearted but with a bit more money in my pocket to hand over and keep my father happy, with no surprise on my behalf, when there was no recognition or praise, just simple expectation on his part. I slotted into the family routine and fell back into my tears. I didn't work that coming winter and as the farm work slows down during those cold months too, I was left with more free time than I cared for.

What also wasn't helping was that while I was stuck in the middle of nowhere, Roberto found a bar job and the times that he would come and see me, he would tell me all about the girl he worked with. He would excitedly recount how she was into him and his displeasure at his difficulties in resisting temptation as I was not as liberated as her, whatever that meant. And all the cracks including the fact that I was barely allowed out began to show. My anxieties and obsessions grew, as did my self-hate. I became very jealous and very possessive which only served to push him further away as I was constantly looking for reassurance and he would get more angry and frustrated. My self-esteem in tatters, comparing myself to every other girl took on a new meaning but always had the same end result, with me as the loser. Still not a word to my family who by now thought him to be their future son in law as he had proposed with family in tow prior to starting his employment with perks of temptations. None of my friends, not even Romina, knew the state I was in, what with not seeing each other very often, it had become harder to confide and easier to keep my mask on.

Chapter Six – A Different World

Things got easier the following late spring, early summer when I found a job, working in a bar which, during the day was a normal cafe and in the evening the place would turn into an alfresco disco (the very same one I had snuck to during my time working at the school hotel. I negotiated a wage that although most people then would consider a joke considering the hours I was putting in; I knew it would be acceptable for my dad. This way I would be out of the house as much as possible, I would do a job I enjoyed, quiet the mind (or so I thought), and meet a shed load of new people in the process. Also, soon, it wouldn't have mattered having any free time as Roberto, being a year older than me, abiding by Italian law then, would be summoned to do military service. Although at first this idea of him being sent away somewhere, played havoc with my head, the tables were soon to be turned and set the wheel of change into motion.

I loved this job, the day one was great but the night one was absolutely grand! The evening was when it all came to life...the music, the loud chatter, the laughter, everything. Although exhausted working six days a week I found it invigorating. I became good friends with all the other boys and girls that worked with me and formed a particularly closed bond with two of the people, both a few years older than me. One was a girl, a very sweet girl, with the heart of gold but easily hurt, Anna. Although as I said I was younger, I was very mature for my age and was there to support her, always. The fact that I could also relate to her emotional turmoil certainly helped a lot in making us form a strong bond. The other one was the club bouncer, Stefano. He was a psychology university student who took me under his wing and quickly became my adviser and confident, throughout the time I worked there. We spent endless hours in my car, in the early hours of the morning, after work, discussing as much as I would divulge of my life, his life, and generally putting the world to rights. I was massively interested in people, emotions, the mind and life and having been blessed with a switched on sixth sense as well as a great ability to read, 'feel' and help people, these talks were right up my street. I absolutely loved these times as for most of it, I felt relaxed, accepted, heard and valued. During these precious hours I could be me, no judgement, no fears just understanding. He and our talks remain to this day one of the most special and cherished times of my life and although thousands of miles away, in a different country, with many years gone by and having lost touch I am and always will be forever grateful to dear Stefano.

Roberto, now in the military, came to see me every

time he was on leave but our relationship was getting more and more strained as the tables had now turned. It was he, now feeling cast off knowing that I was 'out in the world'. His jealousy however displayed itself differently than mine did. He would become verbally aggressive, threatening and on occasions would raise his hands to me. This only helped to make me notice the behaviour of the boys that were flirtatious towards me thus overtly nice, and one in particular stood out. The typical bad boy, all the girls lusted over and flapped around him like bees to honey. Could he really be interested in someone like me? Me... Could he really see ME between all these beauties? I was hooked, painfully shy I would go as red as a beetroot every time he approached me but still, I would keep my distance, after all I had a boyfriend.

As the end of the summer approached and having had a great profitable season, the club's bosses added our names to a coach of school children and treated us to a holiday in the south of Spain. I could not believe it, providing I would take a minimal amount on money, I would still hand over my monthly wages to my dad and listen carefully to all the threats he would recite of what would happen to me if I strayed, my parents were actually allowing me to go! Life felt almost good; if it wasn't for the massive guilt trip Roberto put on me. It was like between him and my parents, there was an unwritten contract to make sure I wouldn't miss out on feeling bad, God forbid should I feel carefree and have fun! Of course these were still the days when I didn't know that the power of my feelings and emotions rested in my hands and I kept dishing that power out to them nearly willingly.

Still, beside the angst in my heart due to my guilt of daring to have fun and live a life, the holiday was great; sun, sea and night life. The only downside was the discovery that most of my colleagues enjoyed smoking marijuana, but although a shock for such a purist, fearful girl like me, and having tried to dissuade the girl I was closest to by imparting my wisdom (minimal) of all the possible dangers of smoking such things, I didn't let it bother me. I decided that it was their lives, their choice. What I didn't appreciate however, was the multiple occasions where I was being pressured into joining in. Unsurprisingly I took the moral high ground, and rejected all offers, which resulted in me being the odd one out, and, by the same token, stand out and I didn't like standing out. On our return and with summer turning into autumn the day bar closed and the disco opened at an indoor location but only 4 nights a week. This meant less money to take home which resulted in my father getting fidgety. It was fine for me to work in a night club while the money was okay but now, we got back to "it's not the most sensible" and "What are people going to say?" What I also didn't think helped, was that he started to see some changes in me, one example being make up.

At the club the bosses started to insist that I should be 'more like the other girls', and gave me a couple of suggestions on how to. 1. Be more friendly and stop slapping the customers that have had too much to drink and get a little too flirtatious. 2. Wear a little make up to fit in better with the ambience. I chose to compromise and went for option 2, thus started to put on make-up. The girls would give me a makeover when I got to work and I religiously would take it off before I left for home. One night however I forgot. It was around 4.30 in the morning and as I was driving up to the house I saw some of the lights were on. My dad was up nice and early ready to go hunting with his friends. As per usual I would go through my check list in my head to make sure I would not be in trouble for anything until I realised I still had make-up on. Panicked, I got out of the car and with my head hung down I walked past my dad making small talk, expressing my tiredness and my extreme need to go to bed. Of course, besides having to credit my dad with some observational skills, I was, a very poor liar, and my father spotted me a mile away. I was reminded in no uncertain words, which, if I remember well, were of the likes of " If you want black eyes I can give them to you with a couple of punches, for longer lasting effect." I never forgot to remove my make-up again.

Surrounded by many (of which some really lovely friends), and able to empathize, reach out and help people, who not only I loved, as it came naturally to me, it also made me feel full of purpose. Still however, the void within me was preventing me to feel connected and an integral part of anything. So always with a sense of feeling the outsider I was growing more and more restless and struggling to 'fit in', to belong.

The times at home were truly an angst and although always the pleaser, I seemed to be forever misunderstood. My eighteenth birthday came and went with no particular fuss. Just a dinner at home with a few friends and my boyfriend supervised by my family. Although this suited the part of me that wanted to forever go unnoticed it reinforced my differences, even the simple fact that people generally did something special for their birthday, something different, to make it more memorable and mine was so understated it made me feel the 'lesser' one. As always though I put on the perpetual big smile which, and this still amazes me to this day, fooled the very people that were supposed to be close to me. NO ONE saw through it, no one spotted the pain and loneliness behind that smile. As my eyes really are the window to my soul and I am and have always been rubbish at lying, the words "I am invisible" flashed right before me…

"It doesn't really matter, no need for a birthday bash" I told myself, I knew Romina's birthday wasn't far and she certainly would be doing something more grand and I could look forward to her celebrations. Even on this occasion, dare I say, things did not quite go to plan. Romina's birthday plan was a big dinner at her house followed by a party at a club in another town. All, except the grief I was getting from Roberto whom was ridden with jealousy as he was still stuck in the army's residency, was looking smooth for my attendance. What I didn't count on, was a very sad and shocking incident that happened when my dad went hunting the afternoon of Romina's birthday. A friend of my father by accident, while aiming to shoot his prey, shot one of our dogs instead. My dad was devastated (and here I give thanks), it was very lucky that there were no cartridges in his shot gun as he turned around aimed at his friend who had made the fatal error, and pulled the trigger. On their return as expected the mood was sombre, my dad took to his bed and as always after a major incident or event he suffered from what I now know as panic attacks. At the time however, I did not know what was happening to him, none of us knew, the fact that he could not breath properly frightened the life out of me. I kept an eye on him all the way through, I kept bringing him camomile tea to help him calm, spoke to him to assess clarity while awake and checked on his breathing the moments he fell into a sleep. I was very worried, and I knew I definitely would not enjoy the party, as not only I was really upset about the loss of our dog, all I would be thinking about would be if my dad was okay. I made a decision (oh my!), I decided I would only go to Romina's dinner as she lived close and I could come back quickly if needed to, but I would not go to her after party and informed my mother of it. Little did I know of the rage, the fury I was going to bring upon me when I returned home after the dinner and went to check on my dad. I was met with a hurray of abuse for yet again 'disgracing' the family. I got more of the "What are people going to say?", "They are going to think you have let your friend down because your boyfriend is not here." (Although I have to say with this one, he had hit the nail on the head. Romina's mum made an assumption, and confronted me as I was leaving her house.) And although I was honest and told her what had happened that day, she admitted not believing me to my mum when they talked the day after and my mum was filling her in on the incident). To my horror, no matter how much I tried to explain that my decision was based on his health condition, my dad would have none of it and his shouting resulted with his breathing deteriorating and having even more of a panic attack.

It took a few approaches the following day to help my father see that his reputation was not lost and I really had been worried about him thus acted out of love and care.

A few months later, my relationship with Roberto came to a halt. He had now been assigned to a military base just a stone throw away from his home which pretty much allowed him to resume a normal social life. This however, had not alleviated any of his insecurities and one afternoon, whilst sitting in his car following a day out with his friends, he had one of his jealous moments. I couldn't even tell you what sparked it off as there was never a real motive, he just flipped. These moments were always based on his hypothesising about the future i.e. "If you do 'this' I am not going to be responsible for my actions", "If you look at 'that' I am going to lose it", absolutely nothing I had actually done but he would be menacing and up to my face. On this particular day I dared to stand up and told him that his behaviour was uncalled for and had resulted in him grabbing me by my throat and me fighting to catch a breath. I made yet another decision and following my usual fashion, an unpopular one, I ended the relationship.

I was right my decision was deemed as a bad one (SURPRISE!!!). Again, as I seemed to be glad for punishment and always grab the bull by its horns, the only person I told the true motive for my choice was my dad and although not a total shock it did leave me with my mouth hanging. My dad response was that the poor boy was probably under stress, and if I got a slap or two or the occasional strangulation attempt I had probably deserved it anyway. The lesson repeated, again, I felt I had disappointed the very person I was so desperately try to please and get that so very desperately wanted approval from.

As far as everybody else was concerned, his family as well as the rest of mine, I decided not to disclose any information or insight. I simply told my family that things weren't working between the two of us anymore which in their book meant it was my fault. He told his family that I left him because my head was turned by all the guys at the club, which (although it killed me inside to know that these people would think so horribly of me) I chose to let them believe it. By default, in their book too, this equalled, my fault. Still, I felt that having been the one who ended the relationship warded some sort of punishment and taking of responsibility. Besides, he was quite close to his family and I saw no need for me to bring family disharmony by mentioning their little treasure's aggressive behaviour. There was also the fact that, I felt, especially after my father's input, he should not pay the price for my noncompliance to a less than safe relationship.

If only I learnt there and then that painting everybody in a good light (except myself of course), even when they weren't the nicest behaved people, I might have got some slack and support from my loved ones, not just then but also in future amorous or otherwise life situations. However, that was not the case. I would have it so, that I would allow for plenty more experiences to come my way, giving me the option to stop the martyrdom. Plenty more opportunities for me to turn my back on life lessons and subconsciously send out the unspoken message "Please sir can I have some more?"

I carried on working. By late spring the day bar reopened for the summer so my hours went up and once again my mind would be more focused on work and the brightening of other people's days thus less introspection. Also the money went back up and I had a happier dad. By the end of the summer the 'bad boy' that relentlessly had been courting me, had me head over heels in love. Despite the warning of my confident friend, that knew him very well and would tell me all about their friendly rivalry with their conquest of women; he looked so genuine that I totally believed his love for me. Although there were some romantic exchanges, we never really got together but my heart broke every time I would see him at the club flirting and romancing all the pretty girls. I was always catching myself looking for him but he gave nothing away. Now that he knew he had my attention and interest, he just gave enough every now and then to keep me hooked. I would thrive on a nod or a smile, on any kind of acknowledgement. I remember even writing a poem about him (I would enclose it but it's in Italian and it wouldn't quite translate to the same effect in English).

He was a proper playboy he played the field so well and knew how to manipulate a girl as naïve as me. He was very aware of my feelings and dare I say it, with arrogance, he toyed with me like a cat does with a mouse caught within his paws. I remembered on my 19th birthday he came over to the cocktail bar I worked at in the nightclub, he gave me a yellow rose (yellow for friendship) and told me he loved me. That was the most ecstatic moment of my life up to that point, such a feeling of euphoria and happiness that I had never ever felt before. I was on cloud nine, I left the club that night with a heart filled with hope, joy and an immense feeling of great expectations. The following evening, he didn't even say hello, he went and stood with a group of girls at the corner of one of the other bars in the place…I crashed.

Roberto in the meantime, had started to show his face at my work and trying to squirm his way back into my good books. As ever the forgiver and the justifier, armed with a guilty sentiment and a 'door mat' attitude, I entertained his company, his manipulative conversations and dare I say insolent manner. During one of his visits he told me that he was planning to go and live in England. Now, I didn't see this one coming, I was still very much "Sleeping Beauty" with not even a hint of suspicion in my bones. Of course over the years together I had told him on a few occasions that going away, abroad, anywhere: England, France, Germany was my absolute dream, goal. That is why I didn't go to university and opted for the catering college after all. That is when the inevitable, beautifully phrased question came. In a very casual way, he asked "Why don't you come with me? It is what you always wanted, your dad would know you would be well looked after because I will be there to look out for you...of course as friends, no other commitment of any form... I wouldn't be interested anyway I am in a different place now... just as friends, each other's back up".

Needless to say this was music to my ears, yes there were alarm bells ringing all over me and my sixth sense was screaming at me. Still I silenced all these inner warnings, after all I was miserable, I felt ever so alone and the young 'bad boy' I had fallen for was a fresh reminder of my worthlessness. The day after, while having lunch at home, I approached the subject with my dad. Clearly, I never said "Could I go to London I have been dreaming of escaping this place forever?" I cleverly put it in a way that would really stimulate his interest and curiosity. I knew my dad had a fascination with foreign languages, he had expressed his likes for one if not both of his daughters to learn to speak any language. In his words "That way if someone calls you names you'll know." My sister did her token gesture to appease him by going to a language college but ensured to fail all exams so they wouldn't take her back. She always had wanted to work in a factory, eight to six and two hours for lunch, nice stable income and no worries; she knew what she wanted and she made it happen. Here was my chance. I reminded my dad about his love for languages (and the fact that if I did this, I would recognise if someone called him stupid), I explained that the boy that was good at giving me a slap or two if I needed them was going to be there, just in case (well, maybe I didn't say it so sarcastically). I told him that I was aiming to spend a year in London, a year in Germany and I would finish with a few months in France as my French was pretty good already. I informed him that I would work and study in all places and would be totally self-sufficient and that he would not have to worry about any up keep. I said that the only help I would need to start me off would be for him to let me keep my last wage so I could buy the flight ticket and have some money to pay a few weeks rent while I sought employment, which he found reasonable. Whether he took me seriously or not my dad said yes! My mom just brushed it off thinking it was all pie in the sky and I decided to keep it short and sweet and changed subject so nobody would talk anybody out of it. After lunch when everyone had dispersed I called Roberto and told him I was going. We went to the agency the very next day to book the flight, he paid for both tickets (I would compensate him for mine when I got paid) and that very lunch time I informed the family that it was all set, I showed them my ticket and watched as a 'the bomb' went off. My dad had a look of disbelief and my mum hit the roof and after calling me a few names, ate my father alive. There was no going back, despite my colleagues, close friends (especially Stefano my confidant), and even my employers tried to change my mind. With fear in my head, excitement in my heart and a courage to silence it all that came from I don't know where, on the twenty-ninth of March 1988 I got on my plane to London Gatwick… Freedom...?

Chapter Seven - London

The plane was an experience in itself as I had never been on one before. I was so scared! Yet I decided to put the fear aside and take in all the details of all that surrounded me, within it and out of it. At the same time, I was trying to make sense of what had just happened, it all moved so fast that I felt I was playing catch-up with my thoughts. I had just left Italy. For someone that felt so ugly inside as well as outside, someone that was so repulsive, uninteresting, unattractive, and useless, here I was… on a plane with my ex-boyfriend, to a new world. I had been driven to the airport by a guy that everyone told me was quite partial to me, all of my friends and colleagues (especially my confident), had asked me, begged me, not to leave, and just before I went to go through the security check, my yellow rose 'bad boy' turned up to say goodbye and make me promise never to change. Surreal. Nevertheless, although I can see it now, then I certainly didn't. I couldn't feel the love, the value I was held at, or the emotional bond that had created and had touched every one that was in my life. I was special, and yet, in my heart, I really felt I wasn't. I reassured myself that despite of the fear of the new, this was going to be my new beginning, in England I was going to feel, BE different. I was going to be, maybe even accept ME.

My move to London was the first major proof that what you dream and focus on manifests. Although at this time I didn't even know what the law of attraction was or had any sort of knowledge about manifesting anything. My 'secret prayers, and constant underlining thoughts and daydreaming of leaving Italy and moving away, had done their job and made it all happen. There was no conscious or practical planning on my behalf, or at least not until the very end when I had to physically go and buy my ticket. No structure, no 'step by step' action. Without realizing it, I had moved my critical conscious mind out of the way of my dream and let it come to life. While it all seemed to be 'working to plan' subconsciously, consciously, it was all guess work, a disorientated step after another, I had practically jumped into a new life with my eyes shut.

When the plane landed at Gatwick, it was dark and it was raining, but I didn't care. All of a sudden a feeling of euphoria washed over me, as I walked down those steps onto English soil, I gave a sigh of relief and the words "Ahhh finally at home!" danced right out of my mouth. I could not believe what I had just said, it was so spontaneous and so very untrue, at least on a physical level; as I had never, in my present life, been to this country before.

The crazy thing, was that although I had told my dad

that we had rooms (separate), booked at a house which an Italian family rented out to young people coming from abroad, in reality this was not quite accurate. Yes, we did have this family's address and yes they did rent rooms, however nothing was booked, we just had to hope that they had space once we got there.

Luck would have it that they did have space, there was a girl that had a double room for herself and struggled to pay the full rent and was very happy to have me share, and the same was for Roberto, he was able to share accommodation with another Italian guy. The house was in Victoria, only five minutes from one of London's main train stations, bus stations and underground services, all of which were totally new to me as I had never travelled via any of these methods of transport before. The house was a four-story house with a basement. The ground floor, the basement and the first floor were habited by the owner and his family; the third and fourth floors, held two rooms on each, for tenants like myself. There was a communal shower and toilet half way up the stairs and a thieving payphone (it ate coins like a person that had been stranded on a boat in the middle of the ocean for a week and had just been presented with a full hog roast!) hung, on one of the landings.

The focus, already from the very first day of waking up in England, was to go and look for a job.

Although when I arrived I had £420.00 in my pocket, and in those days a fair amount of money, this was London, once I had paid the deposit and a week in advance to the landlord, I realised my time of finding work was limited. I could only afford not to work for about three weeks at the most, after that, if unsuccessful, I would have to be on a flight back home with a big failure sign on my forehead.

To begin with, Roberto and I gathered information within the household, from other tenants as well as from the landlord and his wife. We asked how best to proceed, what documentation we needed, if any, and whether they knew any places we should approach first. I noted it all down, agencies' names, addresses, which step to take and in what order. Also, contact names of people working for agencies that previous tenants and present ones had found useful, especially those dealing in the catering industry and most importantly, how and where to go and register for a national insurance number. Over the following days we followed all leads and registered with as many agencies as possible, as well as walking directly into any Italian restaurant we found on our way and ask the proprietors whether they required a waiter/waitress, dish washer, a cleaner, anything. I soon realised that my lack of knowledge of the English language was a massive deterrent for employment, after all a handful of English words and the inability of putting them together was very little of a selling point, regardless of how much of a hard worker I was. Days passed and no calls came my way. Roberto got a phone call after a week or so, even though his English was also non-existent, in those days it was much easier to get a job for a man, especially in the Italian community. He was quick to reassure me that he would support us both for as long as I was without a job, however, there was no way I would accept this offer. Regardless of how naïve I was, or how many alarm bells I was prepared to ignore, I knew that this would be his way of 'owning' me. He was already showing signs of possession and ownership every time we were in environments that included other male company. There was no way I was going to take his offer, besides, I was far too proud.

While the job hunt was taking place the girl I was sharing with left. Roberto (I later found out via the landlady), orchestrated it so, while having a conversation with the landlord and the guy he shared with, that I should move in to share with him. He enforced the point that, it would be too much for me to afford a room by myself while I had no work. To me it was sold as: - "the tenant I share with wants a room all by himself again and as you know me, and you know you can trust me, we thought you wouldn't mind sharing with me. My roommate and I thought it would make your cash last longer while you find a job". I smelled a rat a mile away but my fears of having to go home where growing and my spirit was falling. Also, maybe due to my feeling of worthlessness showing its head more and more, I told myself that maybe it wouldn't be all so bad if him and I got back together eventually. Our families would be happy and surely I could make the relationship so good that I would keep him happy, so happy and reassured that he would never be jealous again... whispering to myself, "who knows, maybe my dad was right, maybe it had all been my fault". I accepted the swap.

Things kept ticking along until one day, to my horror I came home from visiting one of the agencies to find the room door open. I knew Roberto was at work so I realized immediately that we had a break in. The last of my money had gone, all but £20 how kind of the thief to leave me something to live on. It would have had to be an inside job, one of the people who lived in the house, someone that new my whereabouts. Most of us tenants got together in each other's room pretty much every day for chats, drinks and mini parties. I was numb with sadness and panic, I willed it so much for a job to come my way, anything…cooking, waitressing, cleaning, shredding paper…absolutely anything. The day after, to my astonishment, the so awaited phone call arrived and I was employed as a cashier in a very posh Italian restaurant. I was amazed and on cloud nine again, their previous employee had just left them and with the recommendation of the agency I was registered with, as well as those of Roberto who worked there, they were happy give me a go. I would be sat behind a wall and I wouldn't have to speak to anyone, other than the Italian waiters that brought me the tables' bills. Result! No going back to Italy just yet.

My life quickly fell into a routine, I was working restaurant hours, lunch times and evenings. In the afternoons, I went to a school, subsidised by the Italian government, to learn English, socialised at the house late in the evenings, went to nightclubs at the week end and out for excursions on days off. One of my highlights which I remember vividly today, was opening a bank account and having a cheque book. I felt so empowered and so in control! All finances up to now had been taken care of by my father, and he had never shared any information on the ins and outs of how to keep a good system going or about any money management skills; in the past I had just given him my cheques and never really knew what happened to them. I had no clue about how any of it worked, never mind having to write a cheque! I was delighted with my independence and felt very grown up.

This feeling however was shadowed by the so familiar inner unrest; I remembered my friend and 'confident', Stefano, warning me before I left "It's no good escaping from the unresolved, it will follow you wherever you go" and follow me it did. Despite the fact that I would tell myself "Look Dani, you are doing it, you are free, you can do and be anything you want. Look how far you have come!" I still felt so lonely and so very empty inside, restless and so very detached from everyone and everything. I might have escaped Italy and all that it represented to me, but I hadn't escaped my head, my way of thinking and my self-adversity.

With this mind-set, I had recreated a lot of the life I had in Italy, and I passively 'watched' as I put myself back into a cage. I proceeded to attract negative people, and their drama right back into my life so I could walk back into the comfort of my old habits. I stepped back into the rescuer outfit which reinforced my own attachment to drama and feed, at the same time, my need of feeling needed, worthy and important. An example of this was my relationship with my landlady. She would almost wait for me to come home, so she could grab me and fill me in with all her woes and angst. She would tell me daily of her struggle, of how hard her life was with her two sons, one who fought alcohol addiction and the other one that was hooked on drugs and would steal from her. I would stand there and listen to her telling me how she had wasted her life and I would no doubt be a victim of the same fate. According to her this was what life was all about, pain and suffering and I should not expect any different. No matter how much

I would try and raise her up, she would come back at me with more doom and dark prophecies that she assured me, one day, would get me too.

Although we were not back together Roberto had convinced everyone we knew that we were pretty much an item and therefore he was behaving accordingly. No one was allowed too close to me, friends or otherwise. If there were any persistence in showing interest by anyone toward me, I would get it in the neck. Nobody in our circle would step in to help because as far as they were concerned they were friends with both of us and would not interfere, as they believed it to be "couple" problems. I remember on one occasion, one of his cousins had come to visit from Italy, and as we were walking on our way to show her the London sights, starting with Big Ben, he got really mad at me over the fact that I wasn't affectionate enough and I was showing him up in front of his cousin (and remember, we weren't together). As his cousin, uncomfortably, walked ahead, he picked me up by my neck and pinned me against the window of the Woolwich building society we were walking by. I was lucky a police woman happened to come that way at that time and he let go of me. The police officer quickly came over to check on me and asked if I was okay, but I was so scared of the consequences, I told her all was well. Although she knew I was lying out of fear, and she couldn't do anything to wipe Roberto's smug smile off his face, she warned him to behave and with a sympathetic look toward me she walked a few steps behind us all the way. I will always be grateful to her.

Needless to say, his obsession with 'us' being a couple and me being his possession, was obviously a cause for major distress to me and I felt my feeling of freedom had once again gone.

To add to my emotional prison like state, was my Sunday phone calls home. Every Sunday I religiously had to ring home to report in. This was one of the conditions stated before I had left. Despite my well-meant and positive attitude, despite my happy approach and my determination to keep a happy bond with my family, every time I put that phone down at the end of the phone call I had been reduced to tears. Normally by my mother. I would receive a hurray of abuse on what a rotten, awful, ungrateful daughter I was, abandoning my elderly parents (both of them in their forties at the time) and how I should be absolutely disgusted and ashamed of myself. I was paying money to be thoroughly insulted.

After a year of being in London I spoke very little English, as I lived, worked and socialised with Italians. Even though I had met a lot of people, at least ninety-five percent of them were Italian. This was also true for the English college I studied at, with the exception of a couple of Brazilian pupils, that had obtained their Italian passport thanks to their Italian grandparents, and were allowed to attend this particular college, all of the other students came from different parts of Italy. For this reason there had been no real need for me to speak English. Although the teachers were English speaking, mostly from Australia and New Zealand, I was so shy, so afraid to make mistakes and embarrassing myself that I barely ever spoke to them.

In an attempt to speed up my learning process, although my choice, as always, not very mood enhancing, I began watching the evening news as the language was much clearer to understand than the TV soaps. Also, to help with another dose of 'happy' I began to transcribe a U2 music cassette... that was a challenge!

Having worked at the restaurant for a while now, hidden behind the 'comfort' wall, I decided that it was time to take the plunge and get myself a job where I would have to practice speaking English a little more. My problem wasn't so much communicating in English, it was doing so in front of other Italians, especially those I knew. Also financially, I was beginning to struggle a bit. Unlike Roberto, that kept getting subsidised by his parents, I was totally self-reliant and maintaining a lifestyle of going out every week end on my little wage was proving increasingly more difficult.

Eventually I found a job working in another Italian restaurant, this time as a waitress and this addressed and resolved both my issues for a while, however I soon found out there were instabilities between the couple who owned it which made all positions unstable. It wasn't easy to please both parties when they never agreed on anything and for a pleaser such as myself it was a nightmare. I was very relieved when my landlady told me one day that the owner of a sandwich bar around the corner from where I was living, again of Italian descendants, were looking for staff. I went one morning to speak to them and I got the job working there which was perfect. Better hours 7.30 till 2.30 Monday to Friday and pretty much the same wage as I was getting at the restaurant for all those unsociable hours. Result.

I remained working here, at the back of the counter for a few years, and as work and company goes, it was great, I really enjoyed it. The staff, although it did tend to change quite often as it was made of foreign students, were lovely and from all over the world, which helped with my English as well as with becoming a little more world savvy. The owners, a brother and sister, Anthony and Angelica, originally from the north of Italy were also very lovely. He, a man in his late forties with a great sense of humour and the ability to forget himself and often not very politically correct. She, a petite beautiful, fiery brunette close to fifty with an attitude, a mid-life crisis to curse at and a heart of gold. Then there was my favourite, Antony's wife, Rose, a lovely, kind, level headed, intelligent Spanish woman that not only had a head for business and was pretty much running the sandwich bar for them, she was also the perfect referee for the siblings' different personalities and very quick to keep a handle on her husband's verbal indiscretions. Pure comedy.

Chapter Eight – Alex (The wheel of change)

Although to begin with, this place, these people, were just what the doctor ordered, again totally unprepared and consciously unaware, the undercurrent of my life had just directed me to the next 'life shaping' setting. It had just given me a stage, although one of solid support, where I would meet the person that would play a pivotal role in my life for years to come. The accomplice to a cascade of events, that would rattle me to my core, events that would make me question my very life, events that were to scar me deeply.

One afternoon, close to closing time, the phone rings and the boss tells me it's for me. Immediately I panicked as no one except my mum had this number to reach me and she only had it to use as a mean of emergency. When I answered the phone I was met with a male voice who asked me to meet with me. He assured me I knew him as a customer and gave me a few clues as a guessing game. Needless to say I hadn't the faintest idea who he could be, and in spite of Rose, a little later, after I had told her what had happened, giving me ideas, I came up with a total blank. All I knew is that I couldn't understand a word he was saying, I later found out that he was from Birmingham, and that it's a hard enough accent to understand for a foreigner; added to the fact that he was on the other side of the phone and I could not even try to lip read made it near enough impossible. Nevertheless, by the end of a hard and troubled phone call I had a phone number to ring him on to arrange a blind date if I chose to.

After Rose had read me the rights on safety and responsibilities, between her and other friends, I was encouraged, if for nothing else, out of curiosity, to call this man and arrange to meet up in a very public place, and that is what I did. We met one early evening outside Victoria station. The strangest thing (or was it?) happened while I was waiting for the mystery guy (I am always early to everything!). An unknown lady approach me and very blatantly told me that the man I was there to meet would be the cause of so much heart ache and pain for me. She added other things, warning me to be very careful and so on, but her first words were so clear, so direct, spoken with such a tone that my mind was paralysed, nothing else was going in.

Those words hit deep, I don't know why but those words felt so real, it felt as if this stranger had looked straight through me and extracted a piece right out of my future. My whole body and mind felt it so strongly that although my immediate conscious reaction was to wash it off and label it as 'the rambles of an ill woman, a demented soul that had lost her marbles' I could not shake the veil of uneasiness and doom that had swept over me. The fact that I still remember it and feel it so intensely now, is testament to the powerful effect of that experience. I still wonder today whether that old lady's words were a prophecy, had she really seen into my future? Because the relationship I was about to embark on, was one that laid the way to so many inner and outer turmoils. A relationship that balanced between heaven and hell, one that awoke so many demons within me as well as paved the way to some sad and some horrid events in my life's manifestations.

When the mystery guy that I had arranged to meet, Alex, arrived, I had my first shock and dilemma. The handsome young man that came to stand in front of me and whom I recognised from the sandwich bar was black. Now that is not a problem per se, but in my ignorance and lack of black company this came as a "mmm, this is new...this is going to be interesting" kind of reaction. To explain even more on how estranged I was to social differences I can relay a comment one of my friends of that time said when I told her who my mystery men was, and that I should be going for a second date. Through tears of laughter she told me that she could not believe that I, the person that could not split hairs between anyone in the black community, in fact in any community that wasn't of white appearance, the person that could not differentiate between one person or another except whether they were male or female, was going to date a black guy. She also proceeded to remind me of all the times, when out clubbing, she had asked me to look out for this particular guy she fancied, and I could never spot him, even when he was two feet away from me. I was embarrassed by this but as I said, it was not anything personal and certainly not any form of prejudice, none whatsoever. I loved the diversity of London, I loved watching, learning and being part of a place that hosts people from all walks of life, cultures and religions. I simply had never been in a mixed society and my eyes as well as my mind where still getting used to the wonder of the grandness, the beauty, to all that life offered, to all that I had not yet lived. As a true Italian however she also reminded me that I was not to fall in love. To have fun, but to remember that in Italy I would be disowned, I would be given so much stick for fornicating with an outsider and God forbid I should ever have mix raced kids! Although I did get what she was saying, not only because in those days (although not that long time ago), as I soon found out, mixed relationships were not approved by either side, but even more so because of my family, I mean could you imagine my mother! All she would think about (obviously through pure ignorance) would be 'the shame'!

Despite the underlining 'reasons' as to why I should not be dating this guy I went ahead and did it anyway. It was fun, interesting and very good for my English. I switched my U2 songs translation to Gloria Estefan's (which was one of his favourite singers at the time) and put the slang word "innit" at the end of every sentence as he did. It was all very exciting but at the same time unnerving. To begin with I tried to keep it so that Roberto did not find out about my new romance, as I knew, it would not go down very well, but it was not long before he did. As expected, all threats came to light, all sorts of insults came flying my way. He told me to call it a day and if I didn't, he would make sure my parents would get to hear about it. When this did not work, as I did face my fears about him telling my parents and called his bluff, he proceeded to lock me up in my room and dislocated my wrist as I tried to escape. Eventually he had to let me out when the landlord came to get me as Alex, whom I had arranged to meet had come to knock for me. He was aware of my living situation, and as I did not show up to meet him at the arranged time, had feared something was not right. I was really distressed, not so much for having being held captive and the awful pain in my wrist but because Roberto was now in tears and I was failing at reassuring him that all was going to be okay without actually giving in to his demands of getting back with him. I did not want anyone to suffer, part of me could not understand why he was behaving like this. He had befriended one of the girls that had come to live in the building and they were all over each other all of the time, I had suspected that a lot of it was for my benefit but I had underestimated to what extent. Although very good at reading people in a general life setting, I always found it a little hard to read anything that involved me especially when it was about getting attention. After all, how could such a nullity as myself provoke such interest. I had always had this barrier that made me shy away from acknowledging any emotions coming my way. I totally believed him when crying his eyes out, he told me that it was all my fault, I made him like that, and therefore I made him take those actions toward me.

Eventually despite avoiding each other, experiencing many rough ups and downs and very uncomfortable moments, he moved out. In fact, he decided he was leaving England for Mexico with a waiter friend of ours and begged me to go with them. I said no.

Although fun and exciting, the new relationship brought a lot of 'hard work'. Being very shy and having an extreme low opinion of myself made meeting his friends and socialising with them uncomfortable. This was not only due to the fact that the majority of them were male, but also that my boyfriend was showing me off as a trophy. A lot of the time, I felt like the outsider, being treated like a prize doll, estranged from conversation or laughed at for my language mistakes and accent. Despite me sweeping these warning bells under the carpet, as time went on the relationship began to show the first signs of strain. He started playing hard to get and I began to feel even more insecure. With this, I regressed into playing mind games and putting on a display of perfect drama plays i.e. "That is it! I am done with this! I am devastated and I cannot go on anymore…good bye (sob sob)" All staged to see if he would run after me and declare his undying love for me. He never did. Head held high, I would run back and, in an attempt to cause him guilt trips, I would scream some abuse at him stating that obviously he did not love me enough. What would follow next would be an avalanche of apologies on my part and all would go back to normal, till the next time. From the little I knew about his family, his mum and dad didn't have a tight bond, in fact their relationship was quite an open one with no evident display of love. His father would disappear for days and his mum would not bat an eye lid when he got back. In Alex's eyes this was trust, true love and what a relationship was about. For me this was an absolute disaster, as on the contrary I was in constant need of attention, displays of undying love and reassurance. With hindsight, and counselling training, I can see now that he also was in need of attention, reassurance and feeling loved. The difference was he had learned and developed, a more efficient, more productive self-defence mechanism than mine to secure it. While he was playing hard to get I would become more and more needy and insecure. I would see any other girl as a total threat. This, at first, suited Alex's ego; it was a fantastic way for him to gain my full attention, keeping me hooked and at the same time boost his confidence. For quite some time he was happy to feed me the idea that I was totally dispensable, here today who knows tomorrow. However, my behaviour soon became so suffocating that he had to reassess and change his ways. Not so much to reassure me or to show me affection, no. He got angry. He would shout, telling me that I was totally paranoid and I was making his life hell. Still, in spite of it all we moved in together, or shall I say he moved in with me. This at first appeased my insecurities but again, this reassurance was short lived as confidence, self-worth, self-esteem and love for oneself is an inside job, not to be built from the outside. My already shaky belief in the stability of my relationship came crumbling down as soon as he got a job working in a hotel, where the majority of personnel were women.

He loved it. He very often reminded me that I was so lucky to have him, that so many women wanted him but he had chosen me. He overplayed the closeness with the girls he worked with just to freak me out, only retreating when he'd think he had pushed me so far it could really backfire, normally on my yearly visit to Italy. As if that wasn't torture enough for me, regressing into an environment of stone age, where, after the first few hours of 'welcome backs' I was treated like dirt at the bottom of their shoes.

Returning to a place where, even though back for generally only two weeks, I was re-introduced back into the chores and dragged around every relative's house (and there were loads) to be told what a disgrace of a daughter I was. Dragged around for the pleasure of being chastised for having left my poor family and to be reminded what a shameful example I was for their own children. Although aware, yet ignoring all of this, Alex would play his games and boost his ego. Knowing my family did not know about him, he would get one of his female colleagues that spoke Italian to ring my house and pretend to be my friend. He would then come on the phone to tell me what a wonderful time he was having with these girls. Regardless, I felt so in love and I fought my demons, all that were tearing me apart- the jealousy, my inferiority complex, my worthlessness, and my angels, all that were trying to save me- the signs, the alarm bells, my instinct and sixth sense... I kept on and tried to make this relationship work, until the unexpected happened.

Chapter Nine – Losing a Piece of Me

Although I always say I don't have secrets this is the closest I have come to having one as, until now, there have been only a handful of people that know of this experience of my life. There would be other experiences, powerful emotional incidents to follow, but unlike those, this one, I felt (and maybe on some level still feel) it was totally down to me, both consciously and subconsciously.

Despite all my diligent prayers I would say every single night before bed "Please God don't ever let me get pregnant before I marry or my dad will kill me" and counting the estimated days to avoid the fertile days, I got pregnant. My world fell apart.

The shock the horror the fear and panic that hit me was like someone had just shut me inside a freezer with a temperature -200 in shorts t-shirts and flip flops. I was frozen and truly terrified. This had just followed an event that took place 2 weeks prior while in Italy for my biannual visit. I had been taken to the hospital to visit my sister's father in law (as it was the obligatory thing to do), and within five minutes of breathing in the hospitals smells I had passed out. I found myself coming back round on the bed next to the man with the doctor that had scooped me up and my mother looking down at me. As it is normal practice the doctor proceeded to ask the general questions... "When did you last eat? Are you on any medication? Are you pregnant?" To this latter one my mother jumped in in absolute disgust and actually, quite rudely, replied to the poor taken aback doctor " Don't be so ridiculous! What a stupid question, she is not even married!". I think something inside me told me there and then that I was but no way could I ever admit the possibility, so I looked from my mother's stern look of demanding and confirmed her statement, straight into the eyes of the doctor, and said "No doctor, I am certainly not. Just tired and my blood pressure sometimes lowers".

This was a game changer however, nobody to fool or to pretend to, this was real and I was alone. When I told Alex. His response was: - "Are you okay? You don't need to worry, it's your decision, I'll go with whatever just let me know". I held back my tears till he left and then I sobbed. How could I be in this situation? How could I be pregnant? What kind of a horrible stupid being was I? And why was this happening to me? Where was God? Why was he doing this to me? Had I not prayed enough! All of these questions to reconfirm power deprivation thus not taking responsibility for me creating my circumstances. Also, at the same time, beating myself up as it was customary for me to do so. Re-running the ever-playing record that I was obviously not good enough to know better or worthy enough to deserve better. As far as I was concerned I was a sinner whom had got her comeuppance, and now? Now I knew what I wanted, I wanted to have this baby, but I also knew, at least with the knowledge, information and damaging believes I had at the time, what I could not do, and that was keep the baby. I was heart and soul convinced that once my father found out he would have killed us both. It was with this conviction, with this dread that I went to the doctor and after he confirmed that I was in fact pregnant, I told him what I had to do.

Throughout my younger years, I never kept control, I always felt 'I had to do' always 'reading' others' wills and wants. Trying to anticipate what others would expect from me. I never really did live my life for me, even though I had left Italy in reality, very little had changed. I had just moved my position on the geographical map but in truth, I ran every action, every decision, every step under the eyes of my conscience, which was my dad.

I don't know about now but then, the procedure was that you had to see a counsellor to discuss whether you were sure of your decision. I remember begging the lady to please, please don't put me through this. I cried and cried telling her not to try and change my mind as I had no other option, I told her that she would just increase my pain. It was either this now or me and baby gone, if I went ahead with this pregnancy, later. All I kept repeating was "my father will kill me... my father will kill me and the baby... I have no other choice". To her credit, the counsellor, although she tried to present me with options, and trying to convince me that although people do sometimes say these kind of things they don't mean it, and are even less likely to carry the threats through (she obviously knew nothing of my dad and the gun incident), she saw my pain, my fears and my conviction and stopped. I was given a date to attend an abortion clinic.

The time between then and the date was lived in a state of trance, beside Alex, which never addressed the subject, in a moment of weakness, I only told Gemma, a girl who lived at the same house, a girl that I deemed 'life experienced' and therefore not too judgemental. To my surprise, she offered to come with me, she explained that although Alex was coming with me, only another woman could understand and give the right support in a situation such as this.

When the day came, I was in pieces, the angst, the sorrow, the feeling of devastation, shame and numbness were weighing so heavily on my shoulders that I could barely walk. When I entered, I left both, Alex and Gemma in the waiting room and I was taken to, what it felt to me, death row. The room I was brought to had six beds and it was all white. Beside the beds and the small tall cabinet next to them, it was almost bare. The nurse that took me, asked me all the usual questions they ask before any operation and advised me on what to do with my clothes and jewellery when I would be taken to the operating room. She explained to me the chain of events then asked me to slip into the gown she had provided for me. She could see I was struggling terribly to fight back the tears and fighting to breathe. With the warmest smile she reassured me that I would be okay, that everything was going to be alright and as she walked away she told me that she or one of her colleagues would be along soon to collect me. I smiled the saddest smile I ever did smile and thanked this lovely woman that no doubt day in and day out dealt with the pain and the mistakes of people such as me. Other patients began to arrive.

The time soon came around for my name to be called; two nurses came and asked me to sit on a wheel chair that would take me to the operating room. They wheeled me to an elevator and no sooner had the doors closed behind us, they began to recite the same medical questions as when I was admitted and here is where I totally fell apart and I really did cry a river. These two beautiful caring ladies tried their very best to calm me down but to no avail, their words simply could not penetrate even the first layer of my attention. I was still in floods of tears by the time I got in front of the surgeon and the anaesthetist, I was fighting to catch my breath when I was told in no uncertain terms that if I didn't stop crying there was no way that they could proceed as my safety could not be assured if the anaesthetic was administered under these conditions. I tried to control my breathing to the best I could because I knew 'I HAD' to do this, not going through with it was not an option.

I woke up very disorientated to the sound of crying, for a little while I had no idea where I was, my eyes struggled to focus. I found myself looking around, trying to find the source of the sound. There was a round clock on the wall, and then the sight of two beds untidily rested around the one I was lying on, took shape. Two other girls were lying on them and it was from one of these that the crying was coming from. The reality hit me, I was in the clinic, I had just had an abortion (even now as I am writing it pains me to use this word). The sadness and emptiness that followed this realisation stripped me of any spark, of any grounding attachment to reality. Automaticity took over, I fought back the tears that silently started streaming down my face and I turned my attention on the crying girl, reassuring her that all would be okay, telling her she was going to be fine... I fell back into a deep sleep.

Next time I woke up I was in the main ward where all

my stuff was. This time every bed in the room was taken and the place was alive with people's chatter, even laughter. I could not believe it. When one of the nurses came around and told us about the operation after care and discussed appropriate methods of contraception, in my dazed state I heard one of the girls say she would now consider it as this was her third time here and laugh it off with a shrug of her shoulders. I on the other hand, I hung my head in shame and became silent to the world, I felt lower than low, I was scum.

When all final health checks and talks were done, me and my new best friends Shame and Self-Disgust were allowed to leave the clinic.

As I went back to reception where Gemma and Alex both waited, Gemma, as she was closest to the door I had just walked through threw her arms around me and gave me a hug. I softly smiled at her making my way to give a hug to Alex, but was met with a steel wall. I quickly stepped back and we left the building. Gemma, credit to her, tried to make general conversation during our journey back home despite the fact that she was very aware of this uncomfortable situation that had just formed. I tried my best to stay with it and be the politest I could be and engage with her, but my mind was racing. Why was he behaving like this? He had told me it was all up to me, my decision! He had readily agreed with it when I delivered him my 'verdict'! What spurred, this bitter frostiness?

When we got back home, Gemma hugged me again and made her way to her room and I was left to face the cold silence of my partner in crime. When I finally did manage to ask what was wrong with him, why was he behaving in such manner, he didn't even dignify me with an answer. I was mortified, and as it was the norm for me, always armed with my low self-worth, I begged and begged for him to answer me. Tears running down my cheeks, maybe waiting to be punished for my actions, maybe waiting to be told, as my dad often did when I had to make a decision, "you screwed up again, it was not the right one!" but no. When he eventually broke his silence and did tell me the reason I was totally astonished and taken aback. He told me that I had not spared a thought for him and his feelings, that I had shown him no respect and had totally humiliated him in front of the clinic staff, when I returned to the reception and had hugged Gemma before him.

I could not believe my ears, I was fighting demons beyond my reach, I was battling with the fact that as far as I was concerned I had just terminated a life, a life of a child that I really wanted, his child. He... he was worried about the order of a hug and the opinion of some people behind a desk! Nevertheless, as low as I felt, I tried to explained to him my lack of thinking before my action and the pain and turmoil I was in, it was no good.

He held a grudge for days to come and I felt lonelier and more depressed than ever. Even when he did come around I had fell into such a flat mood that I was hardly able to speak never mind smile. At work I kept running to the toilet and crying my eyes out, until eventually I did tell Rose, my level headed boss-friend, what I had done. As the wonderful soul she was, she took me even more under her wing. With her positive approach she'd spend hours talking to me and guided me to see the light side of life, yet I was unresponsive. I began to wear large jumpers and pretend to myself that I was still pregnant. My mind and thoughts were stuck on the baby that no longer was, on the family that I could have had, on the love I felt I had turned my back on, all because I was not strong enough, all because I was too afraid. I was angry, sad and I hated me with a passion. With all these feelings of worthlessness I became even more jealous and possessive toward Alex whose automatic reaction was to distance himself. He would be quite short with me after pretty much any exchange of words and would then spend most of his time at work or socialising with work people. With each passing day I felt I was becoming more and more insignificant to him. What made it even more difficult, was that I had got it into my head, that after having done what I had done, nobody else would ever want me and the belief that if him and I broke up, it would have all been for nothing as living, just for me, was not worth it anyway.

Chapter Ten – Desperate for Love

My head was so messed up that I could not see that I was living in a spiral. That *I* was creating this chain and I was going around in circles. That yet again, I was creating, feeding, the very future I did not want to manifest. The more possessive I became the more I would push Alex away, regardless of how much my crawling and begging had empowered him in the past, this was a new level of jealousy and possession and he struggled to cope with it. Full of self-condemnation and pain, and unable to hold it in, one day, I confided in Monica, another Italian girl, friend of the family I was renting my room from. Her immediate reaction was one of judgement and criticism. She came at me from the church stand point, she reminded me that not only I had had a sexual relationship out of wedlock, which although a sin the church, God, would forgive, but getting pregnant and having a termination might mean excommunication (she knew someone who had). This was an aspect and a possible consequence of my doing that I had not taken into consideration, at least not at the front of my mind. I had considered and attacked myself under the aspect of a moral stand point, on the view of having taken a life, of having denied myself of the family I so much wanted, but I had not considered the religious impact. I was astounded to realise that I had been so intently focussed on all these other aspects and I had not even considered the very organisation that had indoctrinated me of the judgement and punishment of God on people that did what I had done. After delivering this brick of a speech, Monica, realising the vulnerable and dangerously low state I was in, offered her support and suggested I went to confession. She explained that, if all 'went well', I would be forgiven and at least one weight would be off my shoulders; if however, the priest would go for the excommunication, I was to run out before he finished his sentence which would make the order void as I would not have been present to hear it. I thought anything was better than the state I was in, I would have done anything that had the promise to stop the pain I was feeling, we went to Victoria Westminster Cathedral. I shivered as I entered and my knees got weaker and weaker as I approached the confession box. No sooner had I kneeled that I was in floods of tears. I was flabbergasted when whilst expecting to be scolded, castigated and thrown out of this beautiful place, the vicar, after I fought back my tears to let my voice speak of my sins, calmly told me to breathe and that all was going to be well. The relief I felt whilst this wonderful soul was talking to me on the other side of a 'window' was indescribable, I could not understand how a man of the church could be so understanding. After reciting the prayers that I was asked to offer as my 'penance', I left the cathedral with what felt like a massive weight off my shoulders and happier tears; I ran to hug my friend. Unfortunately, this state of relief did not last long, as whilst the church, God, might have forgiven me, I could not and did not forgive myself.

That year I went back to Italy for Christmas, only for four, five days; with the hope that, one- it would help to reset the balance in my troubled relationship with Alex, who had now moved out. In his words 'to try and give each other some space', (I certainly didn't feel I needed the space, but, in my eyes it was better than breaking up), two- as ever the hopeful and believer in miracles, that the change of scenery would help me find peace. I was hoping that somehow, although my family knew nothing of the event that had occurred only a few months earlier, there, I would get a sign of forgiveness from the universe... perhaps an unexpected word from my dad that would just simply mean to me that all was fine. Three- I might just get brownie points from the Italian relations for throwing in an extra visit. 'Three', was out pretty much straight away. My sister and I had decided to surprise our mum and dad and had orchestrated it so that she would arrange for me to be picked up at the airport and I would spend Christmas Eve at her house. She would then convince our parents and uncle to come to hers for Christmas lunch instead of having it at my mum's as it was customary, I would make my entrance and everyone would be happy. So much for the everyone would be happy part, to be fair my mum was happy she got quite emotional, and so was my uncle; my dad however gave me a dismissive hug. He kept launching filthy looks at my mother throughout the lunch and kept repeating that my mom was a fool for not having picked up on this 'surprise'. Muttering that, if it had been him on the other side of the phone, when I had called on the previous couple of Sundays, he would not have been fooled. He was not happy and he made sure we all knew.

'Two', following on from the failure of the surprise, that never did happen and 'One' a wolf dressed as a lamb. At the airport before I left, Alex had told me that he had put a little present for me on my travel bag pocket, and that I were not to open it until Christmas day. Eager, I opened it as soon as the clock had struck midnight and I was over the moon, it was a beautiful little diamond ring, I run to my sister and showed her, almost needing to hear that my excitement was justified. I barely slept that night as my mind was racing from elation to a million hellish thoughts, as I followed my usual trend coming up with reason after reason as to why this could not possibly have been a gift of love. The inner message of 'I am unlovable, I don't deserve love' had by now become a crystal clear belief of mine and by the time I got up in the morning I had managed to turn it into a bitter sweet experience. I convinced myself that he must have only given me this ring because I had put pressure on him to commit and not because he wanted to marry me.

The message that he was soon to attach to that gift that morning when I called him to wish him a Merry Christmas was an in-between of my prediction, it was not me putting pressure on him and it was not an engagement ring, it was a 'we are together for now' ring. Bitter sweet. I accepted the promise of 'now'.

I didn't wear the ring straight away as I had not told my parents that I was in a relationship but I promised myself to address this as soon as an opportunity arose. After all, a for now promise or not there was a good chance that the next time I came back to visit he might come too so I had to prepare them for the 'differences' they were going to encounter. That very same afternoon as my mother and I had a minute to ourselves I thought it would be the perfect chance to test the water on her rather than my father. Very shakily, I told her that I had met someone, that we had been together for almost a year now, that, that very same day he had given me a ring and that I was happy. I mentioned however, that I was not sure how she, or my dad as a matter of fact, were going to react to the next bit of information. After 'playing' my mother's guessing game with questions to the likes of "is he gay?" and "Does he wear earrings?" (not quite sure how this one would be a deal breaker), I told her that he was black.

To this piece of jewel of information, she ran through the names of all the characters from the Cosby Show, the only black people she could really relate the image in her head to for shade comparison. She demanded to know 'how black' he was so she could decide whether it was acceptable for us to date. In the end she said, it sounded plausible but she would need to run it by my dad.

The day after my dad told me "Dog breeds mix so I don't see why people can't". The ring went straight on my finger, thank you dogs!

I returned to England with an expectation of change, a hope for a deeper love, somehow thinking that, although being offered as a "for now" ring", this little piece of jewellery was going to fix it all for me. After all, a given ring is a big thing in a relationship, my Italian culture said so... my dad said so. Although my gut was not in agreement, I fed myself a different truth for Alex's words (as I always did when denying any truth that stared me right in the face). I decided in my head that his, were just words, mirroring his outer fears for deeper commitment. I told myself that in fact, inside him, the meaning was much more profound, one of undying love and a forever unity.

Surprise, surprise, except for the first couple of days, where I got a handful of attention for having been missed while away, as my gut had predicted, nothing had actually changed. How could it? *I* had not changed, *I* had not dealt with any of my emotional scars and baggage. I was refusing to look at me, to look for love and answers from within instead of fiercely demanding them from an outside world that knew nothing of me. Again, how could it? I didn't even know me.

Eventually Alex and I moved back in together. More out of convenience than wanting to, on his behalf, or at least that is what he promoted to me. He was still very much of the opinion 'treat them mean - keep them keen' which he knew worked perfectly with someone like me. My self-confidence as well as the trust in the relationship kept plummeting more and more, yet I jumped through all the hoops to keep us together. I even, due to his excitement to visit Italy, and his need to be even more empowered by yet another 'proof of love' on my part, I took him to meet my family. As you can imagine this turned out to be a challenge and an experience in itself with my mother throwing her toys out of the pram claiming that he was "too black!" and the town people having a fun filled day with gossip and general insults.

My heart was heavy, in my mind I did all I could do

to make him love me, to feel loved and yet I felt more alone than ever, I gave and gave from a tank that was pretty much dry and had nothing flowing in to replenish it. I was really losing control, not so much of my daily duties, although they too did suffer, but of myself. The lid I firmly kept on my boiling pot of troubles was starting to heavily wobble and I could not stop the water from spilling out. I did see a counsellor for a little while, after the termination, but this seemed to cause me more questions than answers, more upsets than resolutions so I eventually brought it to a halt. I knew from the very beginning that the style of counselling this woman was offering was not appropriate to my needs and personality, yet I carried on seeing her. I kept throwing money into it and going through the motions as yet again, I found myself worrying about her feelings, not wanting her to think she was not doing a good job. The reality though was that her silences and the 'mirroring' technique she was using and never strayed from, followed a book practice which left it to me to judge and interpret my own words. As a result, this only served to reflect, to magnify, and reinforce within me, self-hate, and a conviction that I was a horrible person.

After this counselling experience, very disheartened, I believed that these were the best colours life was going to show me and I retreated within, refusing, despite Rose at work, presenting me with a number of a seemingly very reputable psychotherapists, to even consider seeing a shrink again. Perhaps that is why now, to each and every one of my clients, on their first session, I give the speech of the importance of finding the best counsellor for them. I tell them to not settle, for me or anybody else if it doesn't feel right. To make sure they are comfortable and happy to work with me and the style of therapy I offer (everything and every encounter in life is for a reason and a lesson).

It took a very powerful, heart-rending dream to eventually make me run onto the settee of the perfect therapist for me.

I can still remember the dream as it was yesterday. I was back in the convent school, although now as an adult. I walked around the front of the building walking between the new children that now attended the school and other random adults. I felt lifeless, empty and hopeless when two 'friends' acknowledging my pain, offered me a tablet to end it all. They made it very clear that I had to be absolutely sure of my decision as, once I swallowed the pill, there would be no way back. After a short self-deliberation, a quick review of my life and fully connected to the pain I was feeling, I took the pill. As soon as I swallowed it however, a new picture formed before me and ripped my guts out... I was a mother now! I had two little children and a husband, they were there, walking towards me! How could this have happened? How could I not have been aware I had a family? Children...I so much wanted children! What had I done?! How could I have done this to my family? How was I going to explain that I had just taken a tablet that guaranteed me death? How could I leave them?! Tears streaming down my face and terrified, I ran to the 'friends' that had given me the pill and asked, begged for a way out. I implored for an 'undoing' potion, anything to reverse my dying option. The answer was clear, no. No way back; what was done could not be undone. The devastation, the horror the pain I felt hugging my unaware children and saying my goodbyes to them, was so much more painful and intense of all the years of sadness in the life I had reviewed before swallowing death added together. The dream ended with me walking out of the convent gates, stripped down to wearing rags, joining a line of what seemed like thousands of others that like me had chosen the 'way out'. Feeling totally hollow, with my heart in tatters, accompanied by the two 'friends' and others like them delivering whip lashes upon us, I began my walk to death.

What a message from my subconscious! What a wakeup call! Committing suicide in a different realm, in a dream state. Through a dream, I had just had my eyes opened to the beauty of life, to how much life can offer; I had just been shown how much I had to live for. Yet, that very following morning, in my awakened state, I saw none of it. It scared me so much, this dream, in my consciousness, had just brought home to me how low I had fallen, how vulnerable my state of mind really was. I was not able to shake the dream off all day, it felt so real, so that afternoon I picked up the number of the seemingly good therapist my boss at work had given me, and made an appointment to see her. There are always signs to help us see the path.

Crossing paths with the right person, a life changer. Elizabeth was exactly who I needed at the time. I am not going to lie, it was hard work as the therapy reopened, and allowed my deepest, old and current wounds, to bleed me dry. However, unlike the other therapist, this great woman, was also 'teaching' me how to close them when the learning was done and the healing could then occur. With her, through counselling and hypnotherapy, I learned tools and techniques that helped me put to bed a lot of fears, painful memories, unfounded guilty feelings and weights and responsibilities that were never mine to carry. Most of all, she helped me, guided me, to discover me. With time, I began to grow in confidence, I became stronger and started believing that I too was worthy in this life. Furthermore, the belief of not being enough that had set in and reinforced by the mental manipulation, subtle abuse and constant put downs ignorantly dished out by the 'responsible' adults that had raised me, was slowly losing its power. I began to unpack from the heavy load I had been, unwarily carrying on my shoulders, even my mother's words "I'd rather have had a bunch of thorns than a child like you" began to fade away into nothingness.

I began to bring my boyfriend, as well as other people, down from the pedestals I had put them on and raised myself up to an equal level (or there about, old habits die hard!). Through Elizabeth's suggestion, I wrote a letter home telling my parents of the angst I was feeling every time I was calling home due to the tirade of undeserving verbal abuse I was getting from them. I told them that if this was to carry on I would stop ringing. My mother's immediate reaction, when I told her to expect a letter from me, was a mixture of questions, accusations and insults: - "Are you pregnant? You are, aren't you?! I knew it! You were always going to mess things up!".

To my astonishment, however, when they actually did get the letter, the abuse subsided tremendously, only limited to when my mum could not really 'help it'. I also stopped blaming every other girl in my head for attracting Alex's attention and realized, (and I told him so) that his head could not be turned without his permission, that he was the one in a relationship with me not the girls. Ending my message with "The responsibility of respect and loyalty toward me rests with you".

As the love and understanding of myself rose and I put the new learnt techniques into practice, I felt a little bit more in control, and although there were many challenges and un-ironed creases, life became more manageable for a while. As time went by, even though on a physical practical level I was still on a path of self-destruction with an appalling diet exclusive of chocolate and crisps and an occasional treat of pop corn and or chips, as well as smoking a little too much; emotionally, I learnt to show myself more respect. Although only in small steps, I began to take me into consideration a bit more. I started to acknowledge that I had a say too, that I was not just a passenger in this life.

It took a long time, but eventually my awareness that the relationship with my boyfriend was very one-sided, and it did not sit right with me anymore. I could no longer ignore the fact that we did want very different things. That it was only due to my need to 'keep him', my need to make everything work, thus living it fully on his terms, that this relationship was still going. So eventually, despite being in pieces inside, as I felt very much in love with him, and (I can see now with hindsight), very emotionally dependant and not yet emotionally ready to cut ties, I called it a day. I made this decision a little while after I stopped therapy, so a bit wobbly on my techniques of manifestations and application of common sense whilst learning to 'fly solo'. When 'Let's give one another space' became more and more a feature in my boyfriend's speech, so much so in fact that a common friend suggested to me I should send him to the London planetarium. I embraced her words and I kind of did just that.

By now, my working life had moved on too. While working in the sandwich bar, I had attended a secretarial college, which, after having provided me with the relevant qualifications, and following a lengthy job search, finally landed me a job in a big wine merchant wholesalers. I began working there as a bilingual office assistant, taking orders from the Italian restaurants in London and soon moved up to the position of assistant wine buyer which I absolutely loved. Here I made good friends, lifelong friends; and once promoted to the buyer assistant's position, I was given so many more responsibilities which helped me keep my mind busy too, at least during work hours. This job had me pushing and stepping out of all my comfort zone boundaries as the job involved a high level of social interaction, good knowledge of wine quality and taste attending events, very often representing the company on my own. This world was such a male orientated world and for someone like me was very intimidating. On one occasion, I also got to travel to France with my boss to meet some of our French suppliers. Generally, this would be a cause for excitement and whilst in part it was just that, for me it was also a worry overload. After all, the feeling of not being good enough, although decreased in certain areas of my life, had not stretched fully to the work world and the usual need to impress was not an easy task either. Having to spend entire days with my boss, not just a man but in my eyes an authority figure, was for me exhausting as I put myself under an enormous amount of pressure.

Although always the giver, the listener and the positive adviser, as my relationship with Alex had crumbled I was glad to have really good friends around me, two of them to be precise Maria and Jo. Even though I wasn't sharing my emotions very much for fear of boring them, as my mind was so busy re-running everything that I believed I was repeating myself out loud, I knew they had my back, that I was supported. It's a known fact that when you help others you help yourself so I made sure 'others' became my focus. I was living in a one-bedroom flat in Camberwell, South London, a place Alex and I had been renting from a friend of mine for the previous three years until we split and he moved out. A place that had now become, except for the times where Jo, struggling with her own life's ups and downs was coming to stay for a couple of days at a time, my retreat, my hidey-hole. On my twenty-sixth birthday I had a phone call from my mother, it was not even seven o'clock in the morning. It wasn't so much to wish me a happy birthday (although that did feature briefly in the conversation), but to remind me, as she did the previous couple of years, that I was now getting older and the fact that I was not married was not acceptable. She also made sure to point out that this year was even worse for me, as now, I didn't even have a boyfriend. Thanks mum.

I was missing Alex terribly, although I am not sure what exactly I was missing, possibly just the idea of the relationship that could have been, certainly not the drama that it actually was. I tried to feed myself the same positivity, kindness, understanding, comfort and reassurance I was extending to my friends and whoever I came into contact with. I even reminded myself endless times, through painful mental re-runs, of how destructive and damaging the relationship had been. I re-lived in my head all the humiliating events that I had let myself succumb to over the past years with him. All the buying of expensive gifts which were poo-pooed with a "I had one exactly like this, years ago" or "Definitely not to my liking but I suppose I can change it for something I really like". All the put downs, all the mind games…, but nothing was working and I started slipping into a downward spiral again. The positive thinking and lessons I had learnt through my counselling days where nowhere to be felt, though I have to admit, I am not surprised. I heard and learnt everything at surface level, almost something to recite, but had not let much penetrate my shield. To summarise it I had read the self-help book and skipped all the 'practice' parts. Depression hit again. This time however, there was not the drama of the tears, the having a go at myself, the hair pulling or face slapping. This time it was almost worse. I was tired, I was giving up, I was passive and I just kept praying to God to let me die. God did put me to the test.

Life will keep bringing you the same lesson until the lesson is learnt, I obviously did not learn the value of life, of my life via my suicide dream. Here I was licking my wounds wanting to die…a harsh lesson was to come.

Chapter Eleven – Don't Let Me Die This Way

On the 25th of April 1995, while my Italian relatives were enjoying a day off work to celebrate Liberation Day (a yearly celebration marking the fall of Mussolini after the second world war), I was getting ready to leave work same as any other week day. Following yet another let down from Alex, failing to turn up to an arranged meeting, I declined an invitation to a dinner from my good friend Maria who was anxious to pick me up from the pit I was in. I proceeded to drive home to what was going to turn into a living nightmare evening.

As I pulled up outside my flat I noticed a young man, early twenties running on the pavement, who stopped abruptly as I got out of the car and sat on the wall outside one of the houses on the opposite side of the road, just opposite my place. I kept my eye on him, discretely, as for some reason I felt very uncomfortable, maybe because he was making his attempts at pretending that he was not looking at me very obvious. He looked very shifty, or maybe it was just my sixth sense telling me something was wrong. I quickly walked up the few steps that took to the front pathway that led to my door, got into my flat and shut myself in. It was about ten minutes later, I had just, lazily, exchanged my suit jacket for a jumper, I had pottered from room to room, put the television on and sat on the arm chair, when there was a knock at my door. My first thought went to Alex, who had not shown up the previous week end but at the back of my mind there was a second thought. It was a danger bell with an image of the running man I had just seen outside. I looked through the peep hole but all I could see was, what seem to be dark skin, the back of someone's neck which I thought was a little peculiar as given the height of the hole, it would translate into the size of a little person, a child size. Still, part of me thought that it was my ex playing games, and the other part was the ringing of danger bells. My sixth sense was very much on cue and was screaming at me that something was very, very wrong. For years to come, since that day, I wished that I had had more faith in myself and that I had listened to my inner guidance, but that was a lesson learnt with hindsight and on the back of an horrific experience.

In spite of the fact that there had been other occasions where my intuition had shown itself to be correct, once again I was neglecting to 'listen' and put it to one side, although this time, the warning was so loud that I felt at least, I couldn't fully ignore it. Feeling a need for safety, I put the safety chain on and opened the door. The mystery was soon solved, standing on the other side of the door trying to bash his way in, was the six foot-four black runner I had seen as I got home. To mislead me, he had knocked, then lower himself to cover the peep hole with the back of his neck. I remember screaming for help, although I am not sure if any sound actually did come out of my mouth as no help came. Within what seemed to be seconds the chain had snapped and although I was desperately trying to push it shut, succumbing to his force, which was much stronger than mine, the door was slammed open and he was in my flat.

Over the previous three years, I had taken on Thai Boxing and I had become quite good at it, but for how much, some people think (and I did so too), it would be the perfect solution for a situation such as this, the reality of how these things play out, of how we deal with these irregular situations can vary tremendously. This was not a training session or even a ring where one fights with rules and regulation. Not a setting where you can chuck in a white cloth and call it a day. The shock and panic that these circumstances dictated, had my mind wiped out from any knowledge and discipline, and had me at a loss from moment go. It was my automatic reaction to swing for him with the hardest right punch I could muster, but although I did knock him back and cut his nose it was not enough to push him out of the door or to stop him coming at me. As I stood, frozen, in a state of confusion, with my hand over my head trying to make sense of what was going on, thinking: - "This is not real, this is not happening, I must be on a set of EastEnders or maybe… Coronation Street…yes, that's it, it's not real… it has to be a soap…EastEnders…". Before I even realised what was happening whilst in my 'shocked thoughts' I saw a fist fast approaching my face and an almighty punch landed straight on my left eye. I hit the wall. He was in, door shut behind him his arm around my neck and I was choking. With my feet barely touching the ground and desperately gasping for breath, I was dragged to the kitchen. My head was hung over the kitchen sink and I could hear him rummaging through the cutlery draw. As I started to pass out I turned my thought to God and in my head, thinking this was the end, I prayed: - "God, I know I said I wanted to die, but not this way, please not this way".

Astonishingly, as my inner prayer ended so did my fight for breath as my assailant let go of his squeeze on my neck. As the light and focus came back to my eyes however, I saw I now had a threat of a different kind. He had got the sharpest out of a small selection of knifes out of the draw and was pointing it right at me.

He commanded that I was to move into my living room. As I followed his instruction, I frantically scurried through my mind for any thoughts, ideas, for anything I could do, to change this horrid play that was shaping right before my eyes but nothing came.

Once in the living room, without taking his eyes of me, he closed the curtains that were giving view to the back of the flat and turned the television on really loud whilst, at the same time, aggressively beckoning me to shut up and stop my mumbling and cries. Once he was happy that the place was now secured from the outside world, always keeping the knife pointed at me, he ordered me to strip. Daunted, horrified and terrified, I begged, I implored him not to do this but my words fell on deaf ears. My words did not even have time to leave my mouth that his orders would come thundering over and drown them. Naked and shamed, I was ordered to move to the bedroom. I looked around for something, anything that I might use to fight back…nothing. The only thing, an ashtray, which he had already picked up and threatened to bash me up with. My distress and fear only served to feed his power, and insensitive to how many tears wet my face, undeterred by any of my pitiful supplications, he stood by his barking orders and the inevitable happened. A terrifying ordeal took place.

Although I am now 'over' the event, for obvious reasons, I still find it uncomfortable to talk (or write) about the factual side of this next part of the recount. For this, although references will be made to the 'going ons' I shall be focussing my report, on my feelings and thoughts as well as the verbal communication that took place. I am going to try and describe the event with as many details as I can, although I have no doubt that it will fall short of the statement I gave fresh minded to the police at the time. This is not only due to the fact that over 20 years have gone by since this experience, but also (and for this I am extremely thankful), my mind, in order to protect me, has shielded me from the most traumatic pieces of such an ordeal, by hiding the information from my consciousness.

For snippet descriptions of what happened next (maybe playing for time and gathering courage), I am enclosing extracts of newspaper articles which were released a year later after the court case had taken place:

"A 27-year-old woman suffered a terrifying 90-minute ordeal in which she was raped three times at knifepoint by a man who broke into her home"

"Glen Grant, also 27, burst through security chains on the woman's door and threatened to kill her if she did not do as he ordered, the Old Bailey in London was told"

"He punched and beat the woman, a retail buyer, before raping her and dragging her through the house, looking for valuables he could steal"

"The woman shook and tugged at her necklace as she recounted how Mr Grant allegedly switched from extreme violence to tenderness."

"she fought hard but eventually decided she would have to persuade him to trust her if she was to escape"

"He had his hands on my mouth and he kept telling me to shut up."

"I was begging him not to do it to me," she said. "He said if I didn't do what he wanted, he would kill me. He didn't seem stable. He was just from one extreme to another."

"While Grant was with her, "she was in constant fear that he would finish off the attack by killing her".

Once in the bedroom, under no illusion of what was to come next, again, I whisked around the room with my eyes in search for anything that could help me. Nothing was here either, after all nobody ever prepares for such situations, we always think these kinds of things only happen to somebody else. With the realization that there was nothing I could do to reverse this course of action, at least not without getting myself killed an astounding thing happened. Unable to help myself physically, my mind took over. I somehow detached myself from my physical form.

It was like I was there but on the other hand I wasn't me. To this day, I don't know which 'Angel' helped me through it as from the moment I detached, I found a strength, a calculating inner mind, a 'voice' that started guiding me. I was scared, but all of a sudden, I was strong, I was sharp. It was like someone had taken over my mind and my mouth. I began to press different buttons, looking for any lifeline. I threw random statements which most of, to my amazement, were hitting a cord with him. I watched his reactions and kept my conversation relevant to what I was learning through his responses. Although this did not prevent me from been raped without even being aware I was getting him to personalise me. Zoning in and out of lucidity he started showing a glimpse of relating. The first time I noticed this, was when I said that this could not be happening because I was a Catholic (I have no idea what even made me think of saying that!) and Catholic girls could not have sex before marriage or god forbid get pregnant. He actually stepped away. A look of confusion, curiosity and interest came upon his face. For a short moment, it was like that statement had brought him to a place he knew and for a very short moment I almost felt he had changed his mind. That moment quickly passed. A 'glaze' returned over his eyes, knife at my throat he laughed at me and barked more orders. The ordeal continued. I remember coming up with a few more excuses but with the exception of creating short interest spells, did not deter him from his mission.

When the deed was done, he grabbed me by my arm and dragged me around the room. He began going through my drawers and personal effects asking questions as if he was just a visiting friend. Once he saw a picture of Alex and I, and assumed that he was my boyfriend, he found it absolutely hilarious that I had a black boyfriend. Laughing at me he asked "How are you going to explain to him that you have been with another black man?"

Somehow, I kept my cool. I was still operating via the dazed, mind body 'taken over' mode. I talked to him, still through trial and error but in so doing, by gauging what was hitting home with him, what tone, what subject, etc. In spite of his cleverness and calculating behaviour which would keep him very alert, I began to gain his trust. It took a while, as he would not let go of my arm and holding on tightly, took me with him wherever he went around the flat. Even when he drank from a bottle of water he took out of my fridge, he would insist I drank from it too (as I said very clever and calculating, it did not occur to me at all why the fuss at the time). His altering state of mind became very noticeable when I gave certain answers to his meaningless questions or if I made a comment while attempting to gain his trust. My mind was racing all the time, thinking of the next question, the next conversation, the next statement... constantly looking for a window of opportunity to flee. Constantly trying to humanise myself to him, with the hope it would make it harder for him to kill me should it have come to that.

It was like a Jekyll and Hyde, he would behave like he was ready to kill me one minute and the next he would behave like I was his girlfriend. By now my eye, due to the massive blow it had received as my intruder made his entrance, was totally shut and as big as a ping pong ball. His reaction as 'boredom' set in and realised the state of me was priceless… Not only did he laugh, he then blamed me for making him punch me! (I wonder now if he was related to Roberto?). He then, to my total disbelief, proceeded, in lack of ice, to take ice-cream out of my freezer, and in an attempt to help with the swelling, smear it all over my painful eye. Who does that?

Despite how angry I was, at the time raising my voice to a snapping tone on those occasions I re-entered my consciousness and lost my 'cool', I went along with it.

Regardless from where and from whom my guidance, 'calm' and detachment was coming from, I was on autopilot, I used every opportunity to turn the tables. For how hard it was, and it took all the strength in me I acted as if I was his friend. There were many moments when 'coming to' the full realizations of what was going on, I thought to myself "What's the point, there is no way out of this, and if there is, how am I going to live with what just took place?" and almost gave up. But I didn't. I showed him empathy and told him I understood. I told him about my counsellor, I told him of her brilliance and how she could help him. I reassured him that I would not tell anyone about what had just happened and that I would be there to help him through it all if not for nothing else, I was Catholic. Slowly I did get his trust and although only keeping minimum distance between us, he began to let go of my arm. Still the words that came out of his mouth following my warm friendly speech left me iced. "I can't let you go, I will spend the night and I will kill you in the morning. I am not going back in". Although not quite sure where 'in' was, despite my shocked state I gathered it was some sort of institution, first thought, prison. His words together with the realization that he had been in prison before, turned considered possibility of him killing me into an undeniable outcome.

Hysteria began to surface. I now knew for a fact that win or lose I had to take the risk and escape imminently. I had to, that very evening, while it was still day light and there were people driving about who could help me. I had nothing to lose. Failing to do this was guaranteed death. I had to try, first the knife had to go. As I was guided back into the bedroom (although un-held) fully aware of the knife he was still holding his hand, again guided by my unseen force, I consciously chose to let my hysteria show.   Pointing at the knife I began screaming at him "Oh my God! Oh my God! The knife! The knife! You are going to hurt me…"   or something of the sort, I cannot remember clearly now (I just remember my clear over the top performance as it was so out of character for me to be so in control). I made such a fuss which combined with the trust I had gained, beside him shouting at me to stop yelling, he told me to calm down that he was not going to hurt me yet and screeching the words "Look!" in an act of temper despair (I obviously had pressed one too many buttons and got on his nerves), he threw the knife on the floor! To my relief not only the knife was no longer in his hand pointing at me, but had actually slid towards the corner of the room so a good enough distance from him.

As he went back to rest on the bed in his nature suit, I asked for permission to put some clothes on and he readily agreed with the condition that it would be something sexy! I quickly put on the very same clothes that I had before his intrusion and frenziedly started running through my mind how I would escape. I had to put enough space between me and my aggressor, I had to somehow distract his eagle eye. My immediate fear however was the door, what if through all the bashing it had taken during the break in, it got stuck? He would kill me for sure. I had to get it right, I would not have another chance.   As all this is playing through my mind I found myself looking at him straight in his eyes, and I saw as the penny dropped. Through my pensive expression, blankly staring at him, I had given my thoughts away. He 'knew' I was bolting. I knew, that it was now or never. In an attempt to slow him down or even trip him up, I threw the sheet that was hanging over the side of the bed over him, and ran for the door. It was like a horror movie, he moved so fast! He caught my leg as I reached the door handle, in total terror I kicked and kicked and kicked so violently until he lost his grip and as to my total relief the door was still fully functional, I ran out in the middle of the road.

I panicked as there seemed to be no-one about, no car no people, so I ran to the gates of a business block across the road and noticed a security officer in the booth outside. Holding tightly onto the gates with tears running down my face, I begged, I pleaded with him to please let me in. I told him, almost screaming at him, that there was a man with a knife that was trying to kill me. His response was short and dry: - "No. Go away or I'll call the police". Crying, terrified I looked over my shoulder, back to my flat and I saw my attacker run out of my place whilst still trying to dress himself. I pleaded with the guard to please call the police but to please, please let me in. While refusing the latter part of my request, he did call the police. I heard him tell the police officer on the other side of the phone: - "there is a mad woman here with no shoes on and a black eye trying to get through my gates".

As I remained crouched down on the floor in front of the gates under the watchful eye of the security guard a neighbour from a separate block of the estate, whom I'd never met before came to my rescue. The 'Samaritan' neighbour escorted me back to my flat trying to comfort me and telling me that he would wait for the police with me. He told me that he had seen 'the escape' and the man run away. He told me that he had followed him as having taken one look at me, he knew something was terribly wrong, but when my attacker picked up a metal pipe and tried to hit him with it, he thought better of it and came to check on me instead. The police arrived. I can't remember how may officers were there because by this point, out of danger, I'd let go of all the control I had mastered to keep myself together and alive over the past three hours. Safe in the hands of the police, I was now feeling washed out, completely stripped of any energy, and very disorientated. I just remember the lady officer Sarah; she was assigned as my chaperon. I listen to the sound of her calm soothing voice… I let her take over.

There was noise all around me… people moving around all over my little flat. Questions… lots of questions but the words struggled to come in the right order in my distant mind… I only recall one, only because Sarah was insistent with it, 'who could she contact for me?' Despite of it all my answer was always going to be one, "Alex". True to form however, in spite of the situation he told the police I would have to wait till he finished his shift at work (no, not as the prime minister's body guard as you might expect from his inability to take himself away from the position for this emergency, but as a hotel concierge). Maria my trusted friend was summoned instead and armed with Jo, was there in a flash. I was not even aware they had arrived. They were waiting just outside my flat waiting for the police to do whatever they were doing. I only became aware of their presence as I was led outside after being informed I was going to be taken to the police station for a thorough examination and evidence collection procedure. I remember I was so preoccupied about leaving the flat. I kept telling Sarah that I could not go just yet, Alex was not there yet. She tried to reassure me, telling me that there would be police officers staying behind at my place to let him know where I was. But I was stuck, I had made that my focus of panic. It was only when I saw my two friends, that, at least for a short while, I gave my repeating question "But how is he going to find me" a rest. When I first spotted Maria, she was looking at me with such a worried, saddened look on her face. She had her arm around Jo who was sobbing and barely able to look at me. True to my ways, I stepped into 'I am in control, all is fine' mode. I hugged Maria and thanked her profusely for coming, reminding her she didn't have to. I told her that all was under control and that I would be okay. Maria, a remarkable woman, just let me ramble on and was just reassuringly present. I then switched my attention and mode to 'mothering' as I turned to Jo. She was really crying, I remember she kept making reference to my disfigured face, my swollen unrecognizable face, my awful shut black eye. I made a joke of some sort in an attempt to make her smile. Putting aside what I had just gone through, her pain was my priority, another point of focus. I told her that I really was okay. I told her that all would be fine, that the black eye would soon disappear and all would return to normal. Two wonderful friends, even followed me to the police station. Alex on the other hand, was nowhere to be seen. He made it all about him and did not turn up till I was at the place wherever the police had taken me to be checked. He had caused mayhem with changes and directions, information I was only getting via Sarah and Maria as I was to remain stress free and clear of any dealings. Information that only served to make me more anxious. When he did finally manage to get there I certainly did not get the reassurances and comforts I was after. In fact, he was quite the opposite. He was cold, too busy trying to impress the police officer of his importance to me, and to his work place.

I did not know the place where I had been taken to, I still don't know it now. Most of the information offered to me, that night was and still are a complete blur. Not much really did register with me, I either fixated on something, or smiled and said nothing at all. Anyway, my emotional recollection of this place, is one of 'darkness'. I felt awful. On one hand, I had to undergo the intrusion and unpleasantness of an internal examination, these are not nice at the best of times but under this circumstances REALLY not the best! On the other hand, and this for me was so embarrassing, I felt I had a crowd of people in the hall, all waiting for me and all knowing what was going on during such personal, to me shameful, moments. When in their company, I tried my hardest to look and act as if nothing was wrong. I tried to zone into their light-hearted, mundane conversation but I could not focus, I could not relate, I could not hear! I was ALONE in the pain, fear and my pretences at being okay. The smile I was forcing me to smile was hurting me. Even the massive bubble bath that Sarah had kindly readied for me straight after the check-up, was not helping in raising this thick black cloud that was quickly descending over me.

When all was done, arrangements were made for me to go to Brixton police station to make a formal statement the following day. Discussions also took place as to where I was going to spend the night as there was no way I would go back to the flat. Alex offered me to spend the night at his place, but my friend fully aware of the all background insisted I stayed at hers, and not just for the night but for as long as I needed until I found a place to stay. I simply nodded throughout watching all this as a spectator, waiting patiently for an outcome.

What followed was a string of visits to the police station. The first one was to make a very long, detailed statement. I met with Sarah, she guided me to a room of the CID department and there, we spent hours thrashing out my statement. I talked and she wrote. Not an easy task on both parts, as you can imagine. As I recounted the incident, I was reliving each part as the images of what I had just lived through formed more and more clearly in my head. What I also found difficult, was that I had to tell it slowly, giving Sarah the chance to write it down. I am not too sure why it had to be hand written, but the longer I had to dwell on the details of it all, the more a sense of shame and self-disgust took hold. No matter how small, every time she made an error, I had to initial it to say I was aware of it and that it was duly rectified to the correct version. It all took so long that I even managed to get a parking ticket whilst in the police station! Still the department saw the funny side of it and came up trumps, they took care of it for me. From the very same night of the attack a massive hunt was launched for my attacker.

What they had not realised at the time however that they already had him in custody. Apparently as he had run home after fleeing my apartment, he had told his mum he had done something very bad AGAIN! And refusing to hear about it, she had taken him straight to Brixton police station. This called for an ID parade.

Again, no recollection of where this was. When I got there, there were other people, some faces I recognised, from the police force, most of the others however I did not. I was wearing a set of dark sunglasses which I had recently bought to try and cover my huge, now multi-coloured mashed up eye, and whilst they did not fully hide my shiner, they did a good job. Still I could not help feeling people were staring at me and I was relieved when I was asked to follow an official to a different room. I was taken to an adjacent room, it had a narrow corridor with a small desk on the side as you entered, and although the outer wall was a normal wall, the inner one was made of glass. Through it I could see into another room, the 'id' room. The official, explained that it was in this room that the suspect would be lined up together with other chosen citizens. I was told that although I could see him, he would not be able to see me as the other side of the glass I was looking through, was actually a reflective mirror. He must have seen the horror and lack of trust in my face and as my breathing started to become uneven, he encouraged me to go and have a look for myself. An offer that I was not letting him make twice. Furtively I walked to the end of the narrow corridor and made my way into the room. My anxiety was not appeased, as although I could see the mirror, I could not fully ascertain the inability to see through it as the officer had followed me into the room. After a couple of erratic "But how do I know for certain!" The patient man stepped back into the corridor and walked up and down. I looked very carefully from all angles and decided that it was safe. 'He', if he was there, would not see me. As I exited the room and was back into the corridor, the officer told me what was to happen next and what was expected of me. For now, I was to return back into the main room where all the other people were, when my name was called I was to comeback, enter the corridor and stand by the officer. The men would come in from a door inside the 'id' room and line up against the wall, each of them carrying a number. I would then walk all the way to the end of the corridor (even if I were to spot the suspect half way through), looking at each person, then come back to the officer's desk, give him the suspect's number and leave. I went back into the room and waited. I was nervous, anxious and felt extremely annoyed by my surroundings. While I was in this room I was approached by a couple of young girls. I could not make out what they were doing there as they seemed pretty happy and excited. I felt this to be quiet out of place behaviour for this particular environment especially as I assumed they were there for the same reasons as me. My assumptions were correct as one of the girls asked me if I was there to identify a particular person, which putting together information the police had given us, was the same one for all witnesses in that room. When I admitted I was, she confirmed that they were too, and unsolicited, she filled me in on how they came into contact with him. What followed was an avalanche of questions about me...Had he given me the shiner I was concealing but still visible under my glasses... what were the circumstances of my case... did I know there were reporters there... would I be giving/selling them my story... I could not believe it, they actually seemed excited at the prospects and attention! For what I could make out, without undermining anyone else's ordeal, of all the violence and offences this man had committed, I seemed to have come out the worse. Although all horribly terrorised, he had not laid a hand or physically violated anyone else but me. I could not even put a sentence together to answer their questions. I think I barely acknowledged with a nod that the 'shiner' was compliments of the suspect. Instead I looked around the room at the other witnesses, male and female alike. I looked at their faces, all I seemed to register was a calm and 'relaxed' common mood. A question came to mind: - "Am *I* insane?". I seemed to be the only one cut up about this, so immediately I assumed weakness on my part and turned against me. Although unnerved I was relieved when my name was called and I could excuse myself from 'question time'. As soon as I entered I took my sunglasses off so that my good eye could take an accurate look. When I saw the men lined up I was thrown straight away. They all wore a white plaster on one side of their noses! My running, inquisitive, logical mind processed it and attached it to the memory of my punching my attacker and cutting his nose, but that was one person! It was later explained to me that to make it a fair id, all the candidates had to have the same markings otherwise there could be a miss-identification if a witness based their choice on the knowledge of an event.

Anyway, the way my mind recorded and stored this experience, was that I followed my previously given instruction to the letter with the addition of uncontrollable shaking and the sombre mood of the occasion. However, the feedback I got from my chaperon, Sarah, who was watching together with her colleagues via a camera link of some sort, differ somewhat from my 'straight forward' recollection. Apparently I had started well, I met at the officers desk and walked down the corridor looking straight at the line-up. Only, when I saw my attacker, I launched myself at the furthest wall, crawled against it all the way back to the desk, told the number and ran out. As far as the police were concerned it was a success, everyone had picked out the same person. There was going to be a court case.

All this must have been very fascinating for my ex who decided to stick around, come to meetings at the police station with me and undertake other practical endeavours providing someone was watching and praised his help and support. Whilst in public he never corrected anyone for addressing him as my boyfriend and assumed all the mannerisms of one, in private however he was not as nice, and regressed to his higher pedestal behaviour. He reminded me on several occasions not to get my hopes up. With my head already very messed up by the attack, I struggled to follow all the mixed messages he was sending. He suggested we should move in together but not as a couple, "that bridge" he said "would be crossed after the court case is done". He did explain this would be only a step taken out of convenience as like me, he needed a place to stay. Still by the same breath he would tell me that he did care for me and wanted to be there for me, look after me. I was so desperate for some stability, to find some peace in my troubled mind, desperate for love, for reassurance, and with a hope to rekindle our old relationship I immediately latched on to it and jumped at the opportunity. He made my life hell.

After a few weeks, my eye got back to its original colour and the eyesight, with the interventions of doctors and technology, was not compromised. The only side effect was and still remains to this date, real pain to the eye socket and surrounded bone structure during weather and seasonal changes.

Although there was a genuine worry for the safety of my eye, what I did find very challenging was having to go through a HIV test. More than the eye sorting, what I found trying was this test. Although both, doctors and police, reassured me that the likelihood of being positive was extremely slim, as the guy had been in a mental institution and sexually inactive for many years, I was terrified. They suggested I should have someone come with me to the hospital and Alex promptly offered and stepped up. That is however, where his good deed ended. Despite the doctor telling him that I were not to be left alone for the next forty-eight hours until I got my result as it is the wait that is the hardest part, as soon as we returned home he bolted. He informed me that immediately after we had split he had got together with a girl at his place of work and although they were now no longer together, he was off to see her. He explained that, me getting in touch after the attack, and him running to help me, had prompted her to dump him. He was now off to see her, to ensure damage limitation and a friendship was maintained. I did not see him again till it was time to collect my results. They were negative.

Chapter Twelve – Court Inquisition

The months that were to follow, were months of limbo, months I felt I was not living, months spent waiting. Waiting for the court case, waiting for Alex to decide whether he wanted to get back together, waiting for updates and meetings at the police station… just waiting. Work kept me on track, or at least kept me on some sort of routine; my friends, when I decided to let them in were amazing, but I was shutting down. Once again, maybe due to the fact I was now living with him, Alex, love, having a relationship, had become my focus. This drove me absolutely insane as the mind games had not changed, in fact he had turned them up a notch. Non-the less, I had chosen to substitute the terror of the ordeal I had survived with the old mind-messing, destructive relationship. I remember further down the line on my way to recovery and healing telling an old friend of mine, I had been the victim of two assailants, both as bad as each other really (advance apologies for the bad language!), one fucked my body and one my mind.

Funny thing is, I was so low that I could not see I had a choice to step away from the latter, that I did not have to live that life, I did not have to play this tug of war game that had come to be. I could not see that I was the enabler of this situation, I was in a bad place and I put up with it all. I remember, every night, for months, after the attack I wore track suit bottoms and a t-shirt to bed, this was so I would be ready to flee if someone should come through the front door. There were several occasions when Alex would return in the early hours of the morning, either after work or socializing with some girl, and he would purposely slam the front door, knowing full well that I would enter a mad panic and bolt. Apparently, this was done so he could desensitise me. Instead of standing up for myself I turned my anger within and blamed me for everything. Not so much as in a manner of taking back control but as a means to beat myself up and put myself down a little bit more.

The police kept me updated with all the new developments to do with the case. Sarah was amazing and there for me any time I needed her with whatever questions I might have. When they were collecting evidence for the case, the police needed my finger prints so they could eliminate them from the rest at the place of the attack, instead of me taking yet another trip to the station, kit in hand she came to me.

Still there were plenty of trips I made to that police station. One that particularly stuck in my mind, was when I was called in by the DI. This was not long after I gave my statement and took part in the id parade. In this meeting, I was informed of whom my attacker was, I was told his name, some facts about him, and what he had to say with regards to what happened at my flat that spring late afternoon. Although the DI was very friendly and polite, as always, the presence of authority made me question my worthiness of taking up his time; this combined with the topic of conversation, made for a very uncomfortable couple of hours. (You may have to forgive me here, as although all the facts are of true nature, some may be mismatched in time of disclosure between what I learned at this meeting and that which I learnt after the court case.)

My attacker's name was Glen Grant known as the beast of Belgravia. He had gained this nickname when at the young age of only fifteen years old, he robbed and raped women in this well-off area of London. I was told that he had not long prior been released from Broadmoor, a psychiatric hospital, where he had spent the last ten years, just days before his attack on me. I was told he was a diagnosed schizophrenic and that although extremely unstable, it was the DI's opinion, that he was very clever. I was told that already from before being released, Grant, during his 'rehabilitation' days out, had committed a series of serious offences, and although he admitted to those plus others the police had not even linked him too, he denied mine. I was horrified how could this be? Why mine? Why was I the only offence that he would not take responsibility for?!

The Independent – 'Whereas he admitted the other serious offences, he denied the rape which came days after he was formally discharged from psychiatric hospital. It is thought he did not want to be regarded as a sex offender'

The Mirror - '...as a sex attacker, he was treated by inmates as scum'.... 'His aim was to earn the same "respect" among prisoners as that given to his heroes - mass murderers the Yorkshire Ripper, Dennis Nilsen and the Stockwell Strangler'.

My head was reeling; I was struggling to comprehend what this meant. The DI explained that I would be the only one out of all the people Grant had wronged, who's case would go to court. In total dismay I asked what the man had said to deny the undeniable. What could he possibly say to hide what took place that awful day. This is where it all became even more surreal. The DI said that Grant had made a statement saying that he and a friend that he and I had in common came to my house to buy drugs! He said that I let them in, but that shortly after, our common friend and I had a fall out which resulting in him leaving while Grant was allowed to stay. In his statement, he told of how our attraction for one another was so great that I was more than consensual to having sex with him. When questioned about the black eye I was displaying, I can't quite remember the details, just that somehow, I deserved a backhander. I don't recall much else of what the DI told me of his statement, partly because of time gone by but mainly because from the moment he told me that I was the only denial, my mind was in a frenzy and was screeching at me, telling me over and over that this was going to cast judgement on my case and that no one was ever going to believe me. Fear, fear, panic! I just looked at the DI and all the words that were coming out of his mouth kept flying right over my head, except a recurring one, I remember...'crack'. This word kept popping up and got my attention as it was new to me thus throwing sentences into confusion. "Came to buy crack", "You did crack together..." For quite a while I let him talk and go on with whatever he was saying hoping that Alex (who had joined me for the meeting), would take it all in on my behalf and tell me again later when hopefully I was not so overwhelmed; but eventually I had to ask. The DI's eyes almost popped out of his head! He could not believe I had no clue that he was talking about crack cocaine or even worse, that I had not heard of it before or know what it was. From his snappy, initial reaction I think he thought I was wasting his time, taking the mick; but when he realised my genuine ignorance, he patiently explained what crack cocaine was and, shaking his head that Grant had stated that this very thing was what I was dealing and taking.

On a separate statement Grant also stated that he had read the daily horoscope on a newspaper on the day in question, which had told him that he would be enjoying a romantic night in with a lover. That is what he was trying to put into action that evening when he saw me returning home.

In one of the meetings that followed, I was informed that the court case would take place in September as all evidence was ready and all seemed to be straight forward. Sarah kept up her contact with me trying to keep me as calm and serene as she possibly could, however, you can imagine the kind of summer I had that year. Although I kept a smiley face and a happy disposition with her and anyone else, work colleagues as well as friends, I was petrified... what if the jury didn't believe me! I would not only be living with the shame and disgust of what I had gone through but also with my friends questioning my honesty and forever doubting whether I was in fact, a liar. By now more people (especially at work,) through one way or another, knew that I was the woman the newspaper and the television news were talking about. That, not only mounted to increase the pressure of this pending court case and its outcome, but also to other demons being awaked. For a start, shame. Having been raised viewing sex as a sin and a dirty act, made it a subject of taboo for me and now here I was in a situation where no details were going to be left unturned for people's imaginations.

Furthermore, feeling already guilty for my inability to stop my assailant despite my Thai Boxing skills, I felt people would see me as weak, useless, not good enough. I was afraid they would see me as a fake; not the strong person I always pushed, aimed and shown myself to be, and say 'Ha! You are not that strong after all... you are nothing!' Fearing they would see me through the eyes and mind I had always perceived my father would define me as.

I was horrified when September came and was asked to a meeting somewhere and was told the dreaded court case I had been mentally building myself up for was postponed. Apparently, Mr Grant had a turn 'for the worse' and had to be mentally assessed which added up to having to reset a date. At this point I am not proud to say I had a go at the DI, blaming him for it. He looked so calm and unperturbed about the set back, not a surprise as it must be a normal occurrence in his line of work, for me though, this was not good enough. Emotionally I was a wreck, I wanted it to be over and done with. I needed to remove this weight from my shoulders, especially as I had convinced myself that the court case was going to bring me closure. I believed that after it I would feel much better, almost as if it all baggage would be left behind the doors of that court room once it had all come to an end (and, least we forget that maybe the 'love of my life' would give *us* another go!). All the anger and pent up nervousness came to the forth and I seem to remember accusing the DI of not doing enough; of facilitating, accommodating and favouriting Grant's needs, a criminal need, over his victim...me. Not nice on my part, and with hindsight and gentle explanations on his part I came to accept that it was out of his hands. Although he applied the law, he was not the law.

Eventually a new date was set, it was going to take place early the following year, at the beginning of February.

During this time my work kept me going and to a certain extent helped to facilitate welcome distractions to my constantly busy mind. Aside from the odd colleague actually turning to me and telling me that the incident was well deserved as it hopefully would now teach me to wear longer skirts, the rest of the staff that knew, were all very supportive, and understanding of my 'time outs' and longer times spent crying in the toilets. My friends, each in their own unique way, were amazing but as time went by, they could not reach me, I was not letting anyone in. Once again I was spiralling down, I could not function properly, everything was an effort, getting up, working, eating, even breathing. Many times, again, I found myself asking "What is the point?" and yet I could not see the answer, I still could not see the lesson. I was blinded despite my experiences, my survival, the techniques learned in therapy I was still fighting myself. I was still refusing to see, learn and grow; I was still looking for answers, and healing from the outside in instead of the inside out.

A small poem I wrote at this time: -

Darkness
Inside of me a big black hole.
It's difficult to understand what made it…
I just know it never leaves me and each day is getting bigger.

Although in previous years I had spent many Christmases and new year's eves alone, this year it was as if they didn't even exist… I do remember my birthday that January though, as birthdays have always been of great importance to me, a must celebrate day, that year I spent it alone. Alex had decided to go to Scotland with another girl, he reassuring me that he would be back in plenty of time for us to go to dinner or do something, on this reassurance, I turned down friends invites to spend it with them and he did not comeback till around two in the morning. When February came the court case finally took place. Although it had been tempting to drop all the balls that I was juggling in my head, awaiting this day I had managed to hold on to my job and not to fall fully apart, two very important plusses, now though, this was crunch time. This was going to be a different level of 'out my comfort zone' especially given the state of mind I was in, the depression, paralysed by the fear of what people might think. I was going to be on 'show', the eyes of the nation on this case, all newspapers and TV channels ready to report. I only had one question "What if they don't believe me?". What did not help was that prior to the hearing, I was taken by Sarah to meet with a victim support worker and see one of the court rooms at the Old Bailey to have an idea of what to expect on the day. I was shown where the judge, the jury, the press, the prosecutor and defendant lawyer, the police, the defendant and more importantly I, would be seated. This was fine but whilst waiting for a court room to be free, as Sarah talked to surrounding people someone commented that a rape case had just been thrown out of court as the girl that made the accusation was proven to be lying. I was very lucky Sarah was there as I hit panic mode. How could this be happening? How could anyone lie about something so horrendous and violent? What chance did I have of being believed now? Surely this would now cast questions on people's minds with regards to victims' honesty? After all, I was always made to believe that rape cases were always hard to prove, that is one of the reasons why a lot of women don't report them. It was me against his lies and despite Sarah's reassurance that my case was different, every bit of evidence backed my recount and nothing matched his ever-changing story, I felt sick. I felt weak to my knees.

When the day came and the trial was to begin, I refused my friends offers to come and support me. I felt under enough pressure to be in a room full of strangers listening to the details of my ordeal and I did not want my friends to be scarred with those images my recount would bring forth. Plus, as I was full of judgement for myself believing this would show me as weak and prove that if I wasn't so useless I would have done more in the initial 'fight'. I feared they would judge me as such and be unable to look at me with the same eyes again. Once at the Old Bailey, Sarah guided Alex and I through the back entrance. The case, here in the UK had become of national interest as the NHS trust's actions were once again held accountable for deciding to discharge yet another mental health patient who had gone on to gravely harm a member of the general public. I had made it clear to the newspaper reporters that I did not want any pictures taken and insisted on anonymity being upheld. I was afraid that somehow all this might reach Italy and having kept my family out of the loop, this, for me, was a definite no no. Once I got through the security checks with Sarah by my side and Alex in tow, Alex was told to go and sit in the court room gallery, whilst I, 'the witness', was to stay outside the courtroom waiting to be called. 'The witness'…I could not get my head around how I could be called that. I had not been a spectator, I had not watched anything, I had lived every single second of that nightmare, and here they were calling me a 'witness'… that really did rub me up the wrong way. As I waited I recognised two other people in the waiting area, one was my Samaritan neighbour who had come to my rescue on the day in question and the other the guard I had run to who called the police 'on me'. I had very different feelings towards either of these two guys. Whilst I was very grateful and thankful to the Samaritan, I struggled still at this time, to have any sort of positive feelings for the guard. I was not seeing the positives in his actions, I was failing to appreciate that he was doing his job and through that, regardless of his wrong judgement of me at the time, he had called the police, which was exactly what I needed to happen. In addition, as everything in life is for a reason, his testimony was what was going to reinforce and confirm my version of events, adding credibility and coherence to my recounts. In fact, I am very grateful to both these men, and although I was not able to do so at the time as we could not converse prior to being called to testify and did not see either of them after, I take this opportunity to thank them both for the part they played in such an arduous time in my life and for taking their time to come to court for me.

As my name was called and I entered the room I went weak on my knees. I was seriously trembling. As I was shown to my stand I took a sweep of the room and saw and felt the eyes of all already present, on me. My assailant was there, staring, I quickly looked away. I found the whole thing very overwhelming and it all became even more intimidating when the usher called the "All rise" when the judge entered the room. So much so in fact, that my first word in court was a swearing word. As the usher announced the "all seated", I, like the rest, proceeded to do so, and when informed that I, the witness, was to remain standing I whispered (failing to realize that I had a microphone right in front of me) "Oh s**t!". The words resonated around the court room. Not a good start but people, including the judge, luckily saw the funny side. Following my embarrassed apologies and the simmering down of quiet laughter the hearing began. When I had first entered the room and took to my stand I had been asked the nature of my religion. Then a confirmed catholic I was given a Bible to swear on that I would be only telling the truth. I was also given a glass of water that I proceeded to spill all over the place every time I took a sip! Steadying my trembling voice, I answered all the questions the prosecutor threw my way, not before I managed however to confuse him by telling him that I was not the person whose details he was reading out. He rolled his eyes as I explained he had got part of the post code wrong, and although he didn't look most pleased at my picky approach I stood my ground, I had just sworn to tell the truth on a bible and the truth I was going to speak (even the correct post code).

The court case lasted three days, and although I can, with the benefit of time and a healed heart, mind and ego, recollect these lighter events, then, to me, they weren't light and they weren't funny. Although having been raised to show only strength thus never admitted it to anyone, I found the whole ordeal absolutely terrifying. I hated being at the centre of attention on a good day, but under these circumstances, and in front of this crowd, words fail me to describe how insignificant, small and overwhelmed I felt. After being questioned by the prosecutor, I was questioned by the defendant and that was not an easy task as it was not only hurtful to hear him come at me with questions based on Grant's false statement, but I also found it infuriating. Although I understood it was his job to do, all I would seem to hear was the words "And I put it to you" followed by a lot of trash accusations. Still, I held my head up high and saw it through. I was not present for the Samaritan and the guard giving their evidence in court as it is legal requirement that one is not allowed into the court room to observe the trial until they have given evidence themselves. I was however present when my attacker took his stand, or at least in part. I was sick to my stomach to sit there listening… watching him lie, and although I lasted a while, there came a point where I could not handle it anymore and ran out of the room. Sarah ran after me. I was later reprimanded by another officer for my behaviour, I was told that although they did sympathise with me for how difficult that must have been, that was not a good thing to do. Apparently, that kind of action could be enough for the defendant to claim that I was emotionally influencing the jury and ask for a retrial! I was astonished and mortified. Not only had I shown weakness I could have potentially made the whole thing a prolonged agony.

By the time the third day, the day of the verdict, came I was a nervous wreck. Still, except for harassing Sarah with one million and one questions on what was going to happen next and thousands of fearful negative 'What ifs', I tried not to show it. That was until I was informed that the jury, whom had retired to make their assessment in order to deliver the verdict, were returning to their seats. This was not because they had reached a decision but because they had a question! I fell apart. In my mind if they had a question, it meant they were not sure who to believe. To me it meant they weren't sure whether I had told the truth and that my fears, of not only being shamed by my attacker's action but also my friends having that speck of doubt about my authenticity for the rest of their lives, could become a reality. Through my panic, Sarah reassured me that this was common practice. She told me that even when the case is as clear cut as it can possibly be, the jury has to go through each and every piece of evidence that had been presented to them (in this case the knife) and 'tick all boxes'.

What also did not help, was that while I was waiting for the jurors to come back out, pacing outside the courtroom together with the police, relevant authorities, newspapers and TV people, some of these took the opportunity to come and 'ask' for interviews, comments and requests for waving my anonymity status and let them take my picture. As I have already explained my reasons why, under no circumstances was I ever going to allow that to happen! I was not going to risk my family knowing about any of this. Although someone did manage to take a sneaky picture of me and my chaperon from behind, outside the Old Bailey, and eventually sold it to a magazine (never did get to the bottom of who and how), I was very careful to avoid any cameras and refused to give permission for using my real name when the papers reported anything. The stress and anxieties of my attacker not being found guilty and me been labelled as a liar, were consuming me and my patience was wearing thin, so much so in fact that the DI took one look at my face and stepped in to remove me from the pressures of the media. He suggested that those arrangements would be dealt with after the verdict but that for now, they (the police), needed me. In the end, it only took the jury three hours to decide on their verdict. We were all readmitted into the court room where, with the police sitting between me and the defendant to avoid any trouble, we waited to hear the outcome. I thought my heart was going to pop out of my chest and it was beating so hard; my breathing was so irregular that I feared I was going to pass out. I could feel Grant's eyes staring at me, as I took a quick look, to ensure safety more than anything else, I saw I was not wrong as I met his cold stare. It was a unanimous decision, the jury found him guilty. I did not want to cry; I did not want to show weakness... but the tears began to run down my cheeks and according to one of the newspapers I shouted "Yes!" I personally can't remember doing so.

The police were delighted, as far as they were concerned, they had put away a very dangerous man. After the verdict, the judge was legally able to reveal all of Grant's others criminal acts to a stunned jury. Taking it all into consideration, he gave Grant a sentence of five life sentences with fourteen years without parole to be served in prison not in a secure hospital as psychiatrists pleaded. What that meant to me was for at least fourteen years I would not have to worry about 'bumping into him'.

Chapter Thirteen – I Can't Feel Anymore

Once the case was considered closed, with the support of the police, I accepted to speak to a newspaper and one TV news channel as long as all precautions were taken to protect my identity. This was all very surreal, so surreal in fact, that I can't even tell you where I went for these interviews. In fact, except for the newspaper reporter who I spoke to on more than one occasion and was really good to me, I just remember shaking hands with folks and answering questions. All that mattered to me was I would be incognito, the shame I felt was too much, the less people who knew me were aware that I was the woman behind this horror, the better. The only reason I agreed to these interviews, was I felt it was my responsibility to use the ordeal I had lived through to help others. Despite my fears, I had an inner urge, a sense of duty to speak up so that I could raise awareness and maybe avoid this happening to others. The call of helping to create a better safer system, to hopefully make people think more carefully before making decisions that could have devastating consequences, was stronger than my need to run and hide under a stone.

I managed to catch the news that night when I eventually got home; they had done a grand job, no one would know it was me and in my deep unrest I saw a speck of good in me for having spoken out despite the weak person I felt I was.

Every evening when I got home after the days in court I functioned fully on autopilot, totally detached from my surroundings, from my feelings, from life. This did not change when the court case ended in fact I was for ever more lost, as the feeling of relief and closure I had imagined the successful end of the court case would bring, simply didn't manifest.

The newspaper which interviewed me, in exchange, kindly paid for an aeroplane ticket for me to go back to Italy for a week. This was following my expression of a need to get away. I did not want to be around the first few days after the verdict as the case, due to the underlying political nature it enlightened, as well as the social impact that it fuelled, was going to be spread and discussed through the media nationwide.

Alex was more than supportive of me leaving even though for a short while. Not only would it give him a breather from the question that he knew was coming, but also because, in spite of not always choosing the best options for conduct, the heaviness of what took place over the past few days would not have been easy for him either. On my part, right there and then, maybe for the first time since I met him, I could not think about him, about us.   I felt empty, and yet so heavy, as always I didn't want to go to Italy but I needed to get away…

I got on a plane and went back to my home of origin and as predicted, I was in this way, shielded from all the news that hit the TV and newspapers. Although I got scared every time the television was switched on the news channel I was reassured that there was no mention of it here. As none of my family knew of the court case, never mind the reason it took place, I could, at least outwardly, shut down from it all. Shame however, I could not do the same within my mind. I wished I could quieten it or raise myself from the sunken state I had fallen into.   Instead of increasingly feeling better with each day I was there, I began to increasingly feel worse.   To add to my feeling of unrest, Valentine's day came and I the self-destructive part of me, was sure to latch on to reminding me that the only man that would, could possibly consider being with me after knowing (or at least being part) of all my 'dirt' was miles away with, as he had often reminded me, lots of girls falling at his feet. I rang him. When I wished him a happy valentine's day, he just said thank you. When I asked of his plans for the evening, he told me that he had nothing special on, he was just going to dinner with a friend from work who like him was alone on this special evening. Knowing in my heart that that was the most pathetic load of bollocks I had heard in my head I convinced myself he had no reason to lie. Once back home to England I resumed the usual routine of going to work and sitting at home licking my wounds. I was hoping for Alex to bring up the us conversation but nothing came. In fact there was another girl ringing the flat on a regular basis. Regardless, I thought he must love me, after all he was still living with me, what girl would be okay in having a relationship with someone who was living with his ex-girlfriend for so many years? I soon found out that the 'friend' he went to dinner with, that valentine's night, was one that would. Every time I told Alex however that I could not live like this, that I still had feelings for him, that I was struggling to heal because of it and that I would start looking for a place of my own he would convince me against it. He would remind me that he was the only one who understood and that he really truly wanted to look after me. He would be a little nicer to me for a while till it all kicked off again. What eventually changed it all was that on one occasion whilst in his mood to show me kindness he suggested we went to Paris to visit a friend of ours. My heart lit up this was it! I convinced myself that his harsh behaviour had been so that I would feel even more elated when he told me we would get back together, maybe even propose... in Paris! Whilst there, when I was alone and away from my friends and any form of support, he told me that we would never be together again. (EastEnders and all other soap operas move over!) He told me that he had had a major scare with the girl he had split up with after I got attacked. He said that the reason he went off whilst I was waiting for the results of the HIV test was because she claimed she might have been pregnant (but turned out she wasn't) and needed to be there for her. He told me that this had convinced him that he did not want children or a serious relationship at that. I could not believe it, all this time I thought it was me. All those times he had treated me like dirt, all the nasty comments made to insinuate that all I wanted, putting it politely, was sex, every time I approached him for a reassuring hug or I was upset... it was never about me being dirt, it had all been about him! His own actions, his own feelings! His own struggle which he chose to punish me with... and I let him. Despite of this realization believe it or not, what hurt the most was that he had almost got another girl pregnant and in my eyes, had diminished the 'importance' that it/he had placed on my abortion. Tears streaming down my cheeks, I did not speak. He left the hotel room as he said he would give me some space. I rang Maria, crying my eyes out and with very little sound in my voice I told her what had just happened. When she finished cursing Alex and telling me what she could do to him if she got her hands on him, she told me to get in my car and with or without him to get myself back home. I told her that I had no more energies and that I wanted to die. She heard it in my voice, I had no more fight back in me, she begged me not to do anything stupid and just come home, that together her and I would sort it. I told her I'd be okay and I put the phone down. I locked myself in the bathroom and ran a bath, that late afternoon in a hotel bathroom in France I really did consider ending it all, it was all too much…but I didn't. I got as far as really wanting the end result but too exhausted to consider the how.

I barely spoke during the drive back, again I was an empty shell. Alex did try some small gestures of 'pick-me-ups' as I am sure even he could see I was scraping the bottom of the barrel, but for me, at this point, everything felt so distant. Once back, I fell into a silence, a total shut down within and without, I felt unreachable not just to the world but to myself. I refused to take my friends' calls and having taken time off I just sat on the floor, hour after hour, day after day, night after night. I could not see any light at the end of any tunnel; I felt so alone again, any way I turned I felt a wall coming down on me. I felt cursed, I felt out of choices. I went inwards and locked the door. I cried lots…inside. Once back Alex had gone back to taking the hard approach but this time except for a few bark back responses for feeling disturbed by his demands of 'Snap out of it' I ignored him, same as I did the rest of the world. It was almost as if I couldn't feel anymore, it was strange, everything was hurting but at the same time I had no feelings, a sea of nothingness. I was not coping and was reaching rock bottom again, but to what felt like a new level of low.

I could hardly breath, I was totally desensitised, lifeless. Eventually it was my friends and having to return to work that put in motion a slow process toward recovery, even if just for the fear of losing my job, my income. Totally lacking in independent judgement, my heart in tatters, I started with the basics, get up, get washed, get dressed, tell the thoughts to shut up, go to work, focus on the work, make minimal general conversation, tell the thoughts to shut up, turn down friends' invites to socialize, travel home, tell the thoughts to shut up, go home consider eating, not eating, go to bed, tell the thoughts to shut up, very little sleep, do it all again the following day. Till my friends convinced me to go and see Elizabeth again. Back in therapy, I began to get back in touch with my feelings, taking responsibility for them for my actions. Learning, where my responsibilities started and where they ended. I began to realise just how much undealt anger I had trapped in me, always the pleaser being angry at others was a no no, but anger for myself by the bucket load. I began dealing with the guilt that was eating me up, some 'justified', most totally misplaced, always blaming me for anything and everything. This time I entered therapy determined, I was not stopping it till I had broken all the barriers, I could not hurt more than I was already hurting. If I was going to give myself a shot at living this life, this was it. It was a long drawn out process. I learnt lots and came away from the depths quite quickly considering the depth of the pit I had fallen into. Still it takes time to change habits, beliefs and ways of thinking, it takes trust and dedication when your ways are so deeply rooted.

This post I came across on Facebook from Beating Trauma with Elisabeth Corey explains the turmoil, inner dialogue and bartering I had going on within my mind to work towards recovery. A beautiful description of our inner-selves at work –

(My 7 Favorite Defenses by Elisabeth | Mar 2, 2016 http://beatingtrauma.com/2016/03/02/my-7-favorite-defenses/)

*Hello everyone. This is the **Inner Defender** here. I sometimes go by Beth, but defender, protector and all sorts of relatively derogatory names have been used. Some days I mind. Some days I don't. I like to keep it as inconsistent as possible. That really gets under Elisabeth's skin. And to be fair, we are a conglomeration of defenders, so inconsistency is inevitable.*

I haven't been a big fan of Elisabeth's recovery journey. I admit I thought the whole thing was stupid. It was incredibly risky to take on the past emotions like that. Anything could have happened. We could have died. Not to mention, emotional pain just isn't very much fun. Personally, I was fine with keeping those emotions under the surface. I mean really. Society doesn't like them. Nobody wants to see anybody cry, including me. I've got better things to do with my time. And if those emotions were going to kill us, that wouldn't make us any different from everyone else walking around with endless health problems. But I put up with her reckless pursuit of the truth because honestly, I couldn't stop her.

But she stepped it up a notch when she opened her mouth about it. I mean seriously. It was like a suicide mission or something. She was trying to get us killed. How many times did I have to show her the death threat memories? How many times did I replay the violent attacks for her? But nothing worked. There she was blabbing it all over the internet. I was just waiting for the other shoe to drop.

And then she quit her cushy corporate job to coach survivors about trauma recovery? What? That is when I knew she had lost it. I lost it. I knew we were doomed. I knew we were going to be homeless. What about the kids? And she was doing this all because of her intuition, her higher self, something she couldn't even prove was real? Crazy, I tell you.

I have to admit that things haven't been as disastrous as I thought. I will even admit that I might have been wrong about a few things. But my strategies worked when we were growing up. Elisabeth will admit that anytime. I kept us safe, so she could eventually take over. I'm not 100% on board with her antics. Sometimes I still think she has lost her mind. But I am coming around a little. In the end, I know she needs me. She tells me all the time.

And that brings us to this blog. She asked if I would write to you about some of my favorite defenses, the stuff that really stumped her. So here goes.

*1) **Confusion**. This might not seem like a defense mechanism, but that is why it is so great. When I get concerned about her direction, Elisabeth can read or hear something over and over again and still not make sense out of it. I know exactly how to make it unclear until she drops the idea for a while.*

*2) **Dissociation**. Dissociation is well known these days. I worked hard to keep most traumatic memories hidden with the inner children. In the worst cases, I could just take over, put her to sleep or send her far away from her body. But dissociation can be used in small ways too. Sometimes it can show up as forgetfulness. If Elisabeth would get an idea in her head that I didn't like, I could just make her forget. Sometimes, she would write it down only to find the piece of paper months later.*

*3) **External manifestations**. No. I'm not God or anything. But energy attracts things. And when she* *would get on a roll, all hell could break loose in her daily life. Suddenly, the car would break down and the dog would get sick in the same day.*

*4) **Body manifestations**. If I really wanted to stop her in her tracks, there was always illness. Anything would do really, as long as she had to rest for a while. And because she was such a willful one, she would often keep going until she got really sick.*

*5) **Sleep Interruption**. A tired Elisabeth is an unproductive Elisabeth. With all that trauma and inner turmoil, a lack of sleep is just what I need to put her over the edge. Anxiety at 3 AM is often just enough to render her useless the next day, especially if she has a lot planned. All I have to do is get her thinking about finances and it is all downhill from there.*

*6) **Doubts**. My favorite strategy was to tell Elisabeth all my doubts. She rarely knew it was me. She thought she was thinking those things. And I wasn't lying. I believed all of these things. I would just tell her that it was a crazy idea, it would never work, doom was certain, she didn't deserve good things, anything that made her question her direction.*

*7) **Paralysis**. There is nothing more difficult for a willful person than to have a list with no physical motivation or ability to get it done. She would sit looking at her list for hours without the ability to start* *working on anything. I know those moments were incredibly difficult for Elisabeth, but sometimes, I had to do it.*

In the end, I did my job and I did it well. I kept us safe. And while the jury is still out on Elisabeth's new approaches, I have joined in her quest for now (sort of). However, I reserve the right to stop the madness if things get out of hand. I mean really. We all know I know best.

My own inner defender and protector – the Daniela within, refused to trust the new techniques I was using to aid healing for quite some time. I had to battle hard to find a balance, to compromise with her to get her to believe that there was a different way of living a different way of growing and it did not have to be through hardship. I worked steadily at putting into practice the techniques I was taught and suggested I put into practice in therapy, but my refusal of seeing and accepting me for who I was, with all the traumas I had lived through and self-abuse I had self-inflicted for years, my refusal of closing doors, meant I did so half-heartedly and with half the trust required. This made for a slow progress. Unwilling to see that this relationship was only the tip of the iceberg which I was hiding behind, living with Alex was my immediate stumbling block. I was using this relationship so I didn't have to confront the larger causes that lay underneath. This was one of the lessons I had to master if I was to move forward. I had to learn to close that door, to stop holding on to what no longer served me and that included this relationship. I had to learn that in order to move forward, I needed to stop looking back and trust that life had my back. I needed to learn that it was my inability to let go whilst life was moving me on, that was causing my angst. It was not easy as despite of him treating me with disdain and very much like dirt (and me letting him), he was the one person I had known the longest in this country, one of the few that knew I was the girl on the news, and my partner in the shame of the abortion which I still had not forgiven myself for. That was a lot of weight I was resting on this relationship, on Alex. I don't question that I was in love with this guy but a greater part for me being with him at this point, was not love, but fear of moving on and the painful memories. This is what happens when we refuse to move with the ebb and flow of life, we dig our heels in, we get stuck and we hurt. Unsurprisingly, I learnt much later, in a letter he wrote to me, that Alex was in a lot of pain too. His 'rotten' behaviour was due to him feeling so guilty for not having being there, feeling almost responsible for what happened to me. For this he had decided that he would be there and look after me now, only instead of offering support and a shoulder to cry on, not knowing how to deal with his emotions, he chose to redirect his anger and punishments on to me.

(A poem by Edwin Muir, that my counsellor had given to me during that time. He reflected my situation beautifully)

THE WAY

'Friend, I have lost the way.
      The way leads on.
Is there another way?
      The way is one.
I must retrace the track.
      It's lost and gone.
Back, I must travel back!
      None goes there, none.
Then I'll make here my place,
      (The road runs on).
Stand still and set my face,
      (The road leaps on).
Stay here, forever stay.
      None stays here, none.
I cannot find the way.
      The way leads on.
Oh places I have passed!
      That journey's done.
And what will come at last?
      The road leads on.'

One day after one too many disrespectful comments I finally stood up for myself, I snapped.

I told Alex, in my usual Anglo-Italian speech quotes "I am not your f***ing shoe cleaner!" (A mixture of 'I am not the dirt at the bottom of your shoes' and 'I am not your door mat). I told him I would be looking for a new place to stay and this time the break up would be clear cut; none of his rubbish demands of staying as friends would be accommodated. His conscience and ego might have had a need for that but for me it would have been too painful and certainly make it much harder to let go. He did ask me not to be 'so harsh' and argued that despite of his relationships with other girls, he really cared for me and wanted to look after me.

Even though a little voice inside me said "Look Dan, it can still happen, he loves you really", another reminded me I was not a pet. I could not bear any more of these daily reminders of feeling so insignificant. It is painful to say goodbye to someone you love but there comes a point when you realise that one person fighting cannot save a relationship and you have to let it go. Something inside me said: - "Enough, clear cut…", and only a few months after the ordeal of the court case was done, I said goodbye to Alex and I moved out. He did try to contact me a few times over time but I severed all communications, I could not handle it.

My recount of this relationship might have shown my ex to be a harsh, mean and an all-round unpleasant person; but that is only because I have been trying to convey my feelings and emotional state of mind. In reality, I believe that in spite of his actions, like myself, he was very much a very lost soul. In fact, possibly even more so. Using the analogy of the two little frogs trapped in a bucket of milk, at least, I was scrambling, grasping, looking to come out. Yes, I picked lots of erroneous routes but none the less striving to reach a higher, safer, brighter ground. He simply dipped his head under as often as he could and kept swimming in the same stale liquid. It is true, I believe, that we all do the best we can with the knowledge and state of mind we have at the time and I have no doubt in my mind, that was the reason he behaved the way he did towards me. I strongly believe our paths crossed because we had clear lessons, messages, to teach to and learn from each other; we were the perfect people we each needed to impart and to receive those lessons. We obviously had the perfect past, the perfect beliefs, the perfect mind set, the perfect energy frequency to drive the lesson home. I truly place no blame at his feet in fact I hold him as one of my greatest teachers, friend, soul-brother that has helped shape my life. For this he will always hold a place in my heart.

It was so that all knots had come to a head during this time. Not only was I still trying to restore some sort of order in my head, by coming to terms with my emotions now that the court case had technically put an end to the attack 'saga' and my longest relationship had ceased to be thus forcing a change of home, to add to it, I lost my job following a company take over where ninety-eight percent of the staff were made redundant. Needless to say, at the time I didn't see this manifestation, for the lesson that it was. I didn't see the blessings, the fresh start, the new opportunities. What I saw instead, was hard work and emotional exhaustion as well as another opportunity to ask myself all the unhelpful questions: - 'Why me?', 'What else can go wrong?' and many other of the sort. I thought the Universe and all in it was out to get me. I did not see the birth of the new life that was being gifted to me, right there, right before my eyes. I didn't recognise the opportunity to think-see-do things the 'easy' way. In therapy the power of positive thinking was reinforced and when I chose to apply this concept it really did make a massive difference. I began to do my daily affirmations (a series of short positive statements to keep one focused on one's desired outcome) repeating daily to myself "I am confident" "I love and I am loved" "Every day in every way I get better and better" and so on to address a full list of positive manifestations that would help me create a more positive outlook. However, yet again, my stubborn old habits weren't giving up without a fight and I was not yet done with learning the hard way. Admittedly it is not easy to see the silver lining when you are in such a tornado of change and you have not yet opened your mind and heart to see and trust the 'bigger picture'. I had not yet developed a faith, a belief, that all will be alright in the end. I was passively angry. It was also during this time that I got a letter saying that I was due compensation for the injustice I had suffered at the hands of my attacker. In my mind, they were offering me peanuts to excuse a monkey system, but my bone was not with the amount of money as I only saw it as blood money and I did not want it; my bone was with the way the letter was written. In not so many words, it said if I did not accept the amount they offered I would have to go in front of a panel and re-tell the happenings of the event for which I was getting this compensation and that after deliberation a new offer would be made which might be more or possibly less than the one in the letter. As I said, I really didn't give a damn about their money and I was not going to contest anything, but the way they handled it filled me with rage. I felt then that not only the system had failed me by releasing a mentally ill person for the sake of getting a free bed and risking MY life for it, but then they were now trying to humiliate me with something that more than an offer actually sounded like a threat. Putting me through another 'trial' if I reject it?! What person who has lived through such horrendous experiences would put themselves through reliving them one more time?! Cross, I was very cross, not about the money but definitely about the principle. I felt they were taking advantage of people when they were down. I was so mad at this, that I even tried to go and find a solicitor to help me sue the NHS for their wrong doings, win, and donate all their money to charities and to all the other victims they had wronged, but no one back then dared take on such a big institution. It was only when my friends, seeing my pain and turmoil, told me I should sign the letter and let it go, that some understanding of my thoughts and actions began to take place. Yes, I believed the system sucked, but I was choosing to engage and let it consume me, more importantly, although I was still not ready to fully admit it to myself, I was yet again, choosing another 'battle' to steer my mind away from dealing with the actual cause of my anger and torment, the attack. I signed the letter and I registered myself on a home study course for psychology and criminology in the hope that gaining an insight into my transgressor's mind might help me accept, forgive, understand… move on. Although in some aspect not a good thing, trying to navigate through all the changes that were taking place in my life, helped me not to stay focussed and dwelling on any one thing for too long. This helped to mellow my usually controlling behaviour forcing through a 'go with the flow' approach. The only constant, the fear of not being safe, the need to bolt and the flash backs of the attack. Unexpectedly one day, the journalist who had interviewed me after the court case was at my door.

As my real name and details had been kept anonymous, people had written letters to the newspaper so they could forward them to me. First of all I was touched that this lovely lady had taken time out of her day to come and deliver them personally instead of posting them to me, and then I was overwhelmed at the beauty and love that is in the world. I got wonderful messages from everywhere, including an English family living in the south of France who had read my story and wrote to offer a getaway holiday at their place. They, like others, praised my strength (I felt quite guilty in reading this as I didn't feel strong and felt a bit of a fraud for this) but they also praised my parents for raising such an amazing woman. This, stuck with me and hit within. It accentuated the two sides of a coin battling within me on the good and the bad influences of my parental guidance and brought reflection upon my consequent life choices.

Chapter Fourteen – Deja Vu

For a few months, I did try the 'let your hair down and have a blast' approach. At the same time, I'd left Alex, a friend of mine had walked away (also broken hearted) from her own relationship and we had got a place together. We drank, we danced, we partied, we clubbed and we went on trips together. We certainly tried to put the hurt behind us and borrowed and tested this new way of life. It didn't last long however, soon we both reformed back into our old ways and looked to find that perfect relationship. Needing to feed the rescuer part of me, needing to belong, needing to quieten that inner persecuting voice of a deep-rooted childhood belief (as well as my mother regularly reminding me on the other side of the phone) that I was worth nothing without a man by my side, I felt incomplete. The promise I made to myself eight months prior, when the court case ended, resonated in my head "I will not let that man win and ruin my life, I will not let the attack stop me from having the family I so much want". In hindsight, this was a clear sign that I was still under the grip of strong undealt emotions and that I had not come to terms with the ordeal. This alone even without the addition of all the other changes in my life, made it not the best time for making decisions. At the time, however, maybe out of a lack of patience or fight, I let the clouded vision lead the way. I met 'Jerry'. I had had a bit to drink, he was definitely drunk. He seemed so sweet, so lost; he told me of a life full of pain and sorrow and sold it as his own. My rescuer antennae raised, I told myself he was perfect for me. There were so many alarm bells, so much anger, and hints of danger, but I wanted to believe his lies, this soul that sold himself as a victim of the world. No doubt subconsciously I recognised this relationship as an opportunity to right so many wrongs, surely if I could fix him I could fix every other relationship that in the past had oppressed me, abused me, mentally or physically. I was going to make it all okay. When, just after a few weeks, he proposed I said yes and within the year we married and shortly after I became pregnant with our first baby. Out of respect of my children, beautiful outcomes of this relationship (who might choose to read this book) I won't go into too many details of this destructive union. Needless to say, however, I didn't make it all okay. In reality I signed myself up to eight years of fear, imprisonment and high anxiety episodes. His life was run by addiction to alcohol and drugs thus resulting in very erratic aggressive behaviour, extraordinary lies and paranoias. During this marriage, I was pretty much estranged from friends and general surroundings unless escorted by him. In Jerry's mind, everyone was a potential danger to our relationship. He feared that my head would be turned and I would leave him; even his own family and my female friends were considered a threat. I was watched and checked upon all the time, including at work, I would get countless phone calls to check I had not left the office for lunch, errands or any other thing. In the summer of 98, in an attempt to save our young marriage, three months after the birth of our first child I agreed to move back to Italy where he believed, being away from the company he was keeping (in his mind the root of his evil), he would be a different man. Considering I have always considered my home of origin my kryptonite, this for me was a massive give. The distress of having to return to live in Italy, to the very place I felt I had never belonged, the place I was so happy to leave behind only nine years before, caused my mind to regress to the same numbing lifeless setting I had experienced in my teens, and my heart and body to ache. To add to it all I was doing this with a man of volatile nature and a proven lack of respect for any discipline or keeping up appearances. Still I told myself that I had no choice, I started to get the feeling that my life kind of depended on it, plus I believed that, no matter what, my baby deserved his father and I was prepared to go to hell and back to make this relationship work (the saying was not a million miles away from the truth). The new life, the new surroundings only managed to keep things calm for a few weeks, till the novelty wore off. He made new contacts to feed his old habits and step back into his old ways which kicked off the abusive behaviour on an even grander scale as he now decided to blame me for making him move there. I slipped into depression again but this time aided by my positive thinking and positive affirmations exercises which I had once again shelved and let life events and old habits take over, I hid it the best I could. I felt suffocated, I was now under the constant watch and control of both husband and parents. After two years of being in Italy, our second child was born. At this time Jerry had moved back to England as he had managed not only to fall out with my parents by destroying half their house in a drunken state, but also to cut all work ties in the area and we were running out of money. After a trial separation, which I eventually found the courage to call, having been totally humiliated, negatively looked at by the villagers and with the promises of my ex-husband becoming a model father and husband, I packed everything back up, got the children and moved back to England. I decided that despite it all, regardless of how he treated me, providing that the children were unaffected and unaware of any ill-mannered behaviour, they deserved to have their father in their life. As expected his promise was short lived but I stuck to my decision. Partially out of fear, partially because of the children, I stayed. I protected the children, and regardless of what was going on behind the scenes between their dad and I, I worked hard to keep a smile on my face and an upbeat environment. The time came however when things could not be hidden anymore and I could not keep his anger controlled in front of the boys. Helped by friends and colleagues at work I attended secret meetings with the local domestic violence officer, and the local council housing office and soon my children and I were put into a secret temporary accommodation. I saw a lawyer who told me (to my horror) that despite of it all, Jerry had the right to see the children and have them for set times, because of his dangerous and abusive behaviour towards me there was going to be a restriction order, forbidding him to come near me but the children were not to benefit from this as regardless if it was through me protecting them, there had not been any events of abuse towards them. Within six months of having gone through a small hearing, which I did not attend as I was too afraid to come face to face with Jerry, I was divorced.

Chapter Fifteen – Finding Me

For the first time, I was gaining control of my life. Granted, every time Jerry was having the boys I was petrified and lost many hours sleep over it. Still I encouraged every encounter, every opportunity for them to see him. Even when he started to swap, change and cancel, I accommodated it all as I was determined to do right by my sons; regardless of the fear I was living in during those times they were with him.

From the moment I left the family home, I gave up my job as while my ex-husband didn't know where I'd moved to, he knew where I worked and I simply didn't feel safe. I made the decision to give in my notice and leave my position. This was almost a blast from the past, like all those years before, it was not just the trauma of splitting up, with that, again, came the moving of home (and this time with two little children), the loss of the job, and just to add to it, this time there was a huge blow to accompany it all, my childhood friend Romina, passed away after a fierce battle with Cancer. I remember receiving that call as if it was yesterday, I dropped the phone and fell to my knees.

As I settled into our new home following the spell at the temporary accommodation together with my gorgeous boys and our lovely dog Tessa, I started to 'rebuild' me. Although not physically, as at first I'd gone really underweight, but psychologically, I began to take care of me, to remove the layers and discover me. Having spent most of my life shrinking myself in order to please and accommodate others, for the need to be accepted, to be liked, I had sacrificed me. I started putting into practice what I'd learnt in therapy. While over the past years I had used the techniques sporadically, often half-heartedly, and more often than not to see me through the hard times, now I was using them daily (as meant to), with passion and whole heartedness. I was now determined to rebuild me, and to be the best guide and example I could possibly be to my children as a single parent. My home was peaceful, my mind was slowly growing stronger, calmer. I was focussing with a grateful heart on all the good and blessings in my life. Although still quite rigid and fearful to make mistakes (still not best at self-forgiveness), I started to slowly lower my guards and relax my outlook. I made space for a lot more laughter and a less rigid routine. Whilst teaching my boys to always look for the good and positive in people and situations, to see themselves (as well as others) through the eyes of love, goodness and compassion, I also learnt to do so myself. Finally, in this more peaceful state, I was beginning to really find me, to accept me and to love me. I was not what had happened to me, I was *me* without all that. I started to live a little bit more in the now and to understand and accept that there is a reason for everything and it is not a matter of assigning fault. With time, I began to understand that it is futile to constantly press the replay button as the past cannot be changed, it's the lesson that counts. Life is now. I started to realize that I was as important as everyone else, that I too had gifts to offer, I had qualities and skills that I could offer this world in my own unique way. All my life experiences were not for nothing, they were my lessons, my qualifications and not just for my own personal growth, and embracing of happiness but to also show others the way. I now had the perfect platform to relate, empathise on so many grounds, that I could help and guide others to see through their emotions. I decided to do a home study course on counselling and psychotherapy. I remembered that qualifying as a counsellor and helping others had been a dream in my younger years, and that warmed my heart; although I had revisited the idea over the past few years I had not been in a position to even consider it till now. As soon as I began my studies I knew this was the right step to take, my life purpose, my calling. I took to it like a duck to water and I loved every minute of it.

Chapter Sixteen – A "New" Love

During the process of leaving Jerry, in the midst of those very many moments of feeling unsafe, I remember praying to God, saying that if he let me break free from this situation I will never even look at another man never mind consider entering another relationship. In my mind, while living those powerful fearful emotions, detached from my life purpose, I truly meant every bit of that unwritten contract I was offering to the universe. However, the Universe, the power that is, unknown to me was probably having a good laugh at my 'simple', blinkered offer as a very different plan was soon to unfold. Yes, I did free myself from that relationship and the 'unpleasant' place I was in; although, admittedly only in part as the link with Jerry was to carry on for many more years as he dipped in and out of the boys lives and therefore mine. Still all considered eighty per cent of the angst lifted with the split. As I grew stronger and raised my energy vibrations, I started to attract new people and situations into my life, and one day, love, not the needy, fixing rescuing kind of love I was accustomed to, but a different kind of love...the free, exciting type, hit me right between the eyes on my children's school playground. Despite of my emotional development, I immediately felt guilty. I was worried, I remembered I had made a pact with

God and I was about to break it. I obviously had not yet fully learnt or appreciated that nothing and no one comes to us for no reason. There is always a motive, there is always a lesson, an opportunity to try again to put the learnt lesson in place and I could see at least two lessons here. It took me a while to realize that it was never about me not engaging with another man or not entering a new relationship, it was about my beliefs and the type of relationship I were to form. One- Contrary to my childhood indoctrination which had turned into a subconscious belief, no mean God was going to come and punish me for not keeping up to a 'contract' spoken out of a lack of understanding for life and consumed by fear. Two- finally forming and living and maintaining a healthy balanced relationship.

Stewart, came bulldozing into my life, and although not fully appreciated by my emotional defences and guarded walls at the time, the best match for me. As relationships go, we healed one another, he too, like myself, had not long broken free from a painful relationship. On my part, with this man I discovered that when you find love, the relationship is not one of hard work, begging or walking on eggshells; but one of unconditional love and encouragement. A relationship where although you grow as a couple, you are still allowed to grow as an individual. I also learned the importance of 50-50, the balance of give and take (one thing that as a giver I found hard to grasp), and how the freedom of expression and the power of communication are the perfect substitutes for fear, anger, arguments and resentments.

The more I grew and practiced positive intentions, the more I raised my energy vibration to a higher level and I was now attracting and manifesting situations that were perfect for me and a new chapter with its own set of lessons began to unfold. I applied and got employed in a school working with children with special needs and autism. This job was perfect for me, as my working hours and holidays matched those of my children and Stewart (a teacher).

Once I started work I kept faithful to my studies and working hard on them I saw them through to the end. Having received the highest grades throughout the course, it was not long till I got my qualifications as a counsellor and psychotherapist which I then expanded with the techniques of CBT and hypnotherapy. I was delighted. Every piece of work that was returned to me was a cause for suspense followed by delight every time I opened the envelope to discover another high achieving grade, so you can imagine how elated I was when I received my diploma and higher diploma respectively.

With discipline and dedication, I kept up with my practice of turning every negative thought into a positive, doing my affirmations and regularly visualising my goals and dreams. With the belief that every thought is a silent prayer, I began to focus on what I wanted instead of what I didn't, a practice that I still maintain today. With these techniques in place I slowly trained and reprogrammed my mind until it became second nature. Suddenly I began to naturally view things differently, to feel different; a deeper understanding and acceptance of my place in life began to set in. All the love, understanding and compassion that over my life course I had extended to others, I was now also applying it to me; and to my total astonishment after all the years of self-hate, I was starting to love me.

Following a short spell of advertising in the local area, I got my first client; and after the initial fears and feelings of insecurity, alongside my school work, I started working as a counsellor. I felt amazing! I was helping people. Everything I had lived through, had proved to be for a reason, for this very purpose and, maybe for the first time, I 'saw' the bigger picture. I saw the woven tapestry of the universe and how it all fits in together. How we all interact and play a part to connect every piece of the puzzle to create the bigger picture in this life. Soon, one client turned into two and then three and since then there has been very little need for me to advertise as it all progressed successfully via word of mouth. Watching the pain, of each and every person that came to see me, turn into strength and smiles, filled my heart with joy and confirmed to me that this was my purpose, and although I still carried on with working in the school for a few more years, I felt counselling was my path in life.

Life seemed to roll from there, my new outlook finally brought balance to my life. The belief that, changing ourselves and our perceptions change our world, as the famous statement 'Change your thoughts, change your life' says, had undoubtedly been a driving force in my life.

At the age of forty-one surrounded by close friends, I married Stewart, my soulmate. My eldest son proudly gave me away and my youngest, delighted, was our ring bearer. Truly one of the happiest days, memories of my (and from what my husband and children tell me), their life. With each year that has passed since then, safe in the peaceful and loving environment that is my family and home, I have grown to discover more of who I am. I have grown in confidence; I have stripped away many of the layers that were hiding and clouding my spark. I have thrown away the fear of not being liked and the need to please the world because of it… I found the courage to be me. Alongside the blessing of my family, I am now living my dream; I successfully work full time as a private counsellor, offering an integrative approach to therapy which enables me to help people on a grander and varied scale. Being able to help others return to their rightful happy state of being fills me with joy and I give thanks every day for my gifts wrapped in the ability to deliver this help.

Chapter Seventeen – An Inner Knowing

Of course, we never cease to learn in life, to discover more about ourselves, and I am under no illusion that there are obstacles on the way; that is the undercurrent of our life, learning and growing. Even when we think we have it all under control, even when we think to ourselves "got it, I am in the now, I have mastered the art of acceptance, the rhythm of life, I hold unconditional love for whatever manifests as I know everything is for a reason and things are just as they are meant to be", there is always that one thing that makes us realise, nope, there's another layer, another lesson, another depth, new levels of being better. As new situations take place, caught by surprise, at times we do step back into our old ways. It is a natural response to return to 'what we know', what has been our way of life for so long. The important thing, I have learnt, is to remember not to stay there to remember why we changed those ways in the first instance... they did not serve us well. In those life situations when, unsuspecting, we create our own pain through the use of ill thoughts attached to very old beliefs, cheated by our own ego, we must remind ourselves that we have only come to visit, we do not live there anymore.

I have learnt that life always guides us and sooner or later gives us the answers. It reveals the lessons in the walk we have walked. It teaches us the importance of flexibility and adaptation as we grow through the many different experiences. It shows us how our thought perception can influence our life. It shows us how different the ways we once saw something as, and what those very things were like, from someone else's perspective. All the times we might have felt worthless and insignificant and yet we were huge and important in someone else's eyes. As an example, only two summers ago, during a convent school reunion, I was told by one of the girls that was at the school during the same years I was there, that she survived those times thanks to me. She told me, as she gave me the biggest hug, that I was the only person that had helped her through, what for her was a living hell. As my jaw hit the floor, she told me that she had never forgotten me, and that she was very grateful for this opportunity to be able to finally thank me. I had no idea and it had never crossed my mind that despite of my own struggles in childhood I had been a light in someone else's life. Life gives us the answers.

Life has taught me that everything and everyone is for a reason. The anxiety, the obsessions, the insecurities, the deep fears, the eating disorders, the depression, the bullying, the self-harming, the abuse, the abortion, the domestic violence, the rape and so on, all experiences that have brought me back to me and made me the strong woman that I am today. Without those experiences, I would not have had the deeper understanding that now serves me so well when helping others. You can't learn that in a book. When my father passed away after years of battling with Alzheimer's a few years back, in times of reflection, I realised that, although seemingly harsh, the role my father had played in my childhood was pivotal to this very moment in my life. My excessive attachment to the family, if not eradicated, would never have allowed me to be where I am today.

I have learnt that although it is easy to point fingers, the reality is that we all play our own part in the play that is our life. It is only when we take responsibility and ownership of our life that we can then, more successfully, direct our sails to our chosen destination. My peace has come with this acceptance as well as with the realisation that we all do the best we can with the information we have at the time. We all have a purpose, a way, a reason, for the lessons we get and those we impart; no one is born 'bad'. In life, no lesson, no person, no interaction is wasted or in vain. We just have to learn to remember to persevere, to trust and to move with the ebb and flow of life.

Yes, on my way, I have crawled, I have slithered, I have limped my way onwards... I have stumbled and fallen into unbearable depths many more times than I care to admit or remember; but I got up. I have very often shrunk myself for someone else's comfort, yet I fought and strove to find myself, and through perseverance I have created and I still create every day, MYSELF. Yes, I have an amazing inner strength but I also have great trust in love and its power to conquer all. This combined with the belief that there is good in everyone, if I choose to see it, has helped me navigate my way through the hard times; I kept my hopes alive. I was prepared to listen, to try everything that had either come to me or had been suggested. The ability to always being open to suggestions has allowed new doors to open thus giving me the opportunities to find, to try different ways and approaches. In turn, trying different ways brought me to new paths and the much-needed solutions. My body no doubt will, but my mind, my spirit, will never lie down again.

I can't tell you exactly when it happened, when the shift occurred. Whether there was a definitive turning point or if it has been a day by day gradual change. Maybe because of the way, over the years I fought for me to become 'ME', but one day I looked in the mirror and all I could see and feel was love. Finally, in my late thirties, I began to feel my love, an acceptance and understanding of myself that brought me a powerful sense of peace. I felt a closeness, a comrade, a 'bond' which I'd never experienced. I began to feel whole. I now see me as my best friend, my best accomplice, I feel a union with my inner self that fills my eyes with glee, excitement, pride and warmth. No validation or acceptance is any longer required from the outside. The validation, the acceptance, and the strength is now coming from within.

With love and gratitude…

Daniela began her journey in rural Italy, surrounded by scrutiny and judgement, searching for love, acceptance and purpose. Her determination and hopes led her on a tumultuous journey that has seen her deal with the dramatic realities of her life. Using the strength and knowledge gained she has sought and found a balance and tranquillity she now channels into guiding and supporting others. Through her counselling and public speaking she is now dedicated to helping others face and overcome their difficulties and demons in life and continues to deliver her message of love, hope and peace.

Printed in Great Britain
by Amazon